THE BIG *leap*

A BAREFOOT GIRL'S JOURNEY

CLEO PILLON

WeBook Publishing
English Edition

THE BIG
leap
A BAREFOOT GIRL'S JOURNEY

To all those who decide to take big leaps in their lives.

We plant the seed of self-acceptance and confidence by instilling **authenticity** in a lucid, profound, and fair way. Like a fruit tree, each individual can create strong roots and expand through instrumentalized and respectful **self-development.**

By transforming themselves into their full potential and embracing a more authentic identity, it is only natural that they will reap the benefits. This **authority** generates a transformation that positively affects not only one's own life but also the lives of all the environments and people around them.

Acknowledgments

To my biological mother, Maria, for bringing me to life and for being such a strong and courageous woman. I don't know a braver woman than you.

To my adoptive mother, Altair, for taking care of me like a daughter.

To my sister Keila, for giving me the opportunity to leave *Maranhão* and pursue my dreams without judgment.

To my sister Luísa, who, at just 9 years old, had to take on the responsibility of looking after three other lives. Today, she is responsible for my business and personal life. My right-hand woman in everything.

To my father, Pedro, for loving me unconditionally. A strong, hard-working man, always concerned about his children's future.

To my brother Rui, who never sleeps a day without praying for our family.

To my son Pedro, for teaching me the value of every moment, for kissing me on the forehead every day, and telling me that he loves me. You are undoubtedly the best part of me.

To my husband, Gustavo, for looking after our marriage with such affection. For strengthening me every day, advising me with love and loyalty. You are a man of drive and determination who spares no effort to take care of his family.

To my psychoanalyst, Dr. Marcos Panizza, for guiding me on this journey through the mysteries of the human mind. Without you, this book would still be in my imagination.

To my friend Igor Oak, the most loyal, faithful, and fair person I have ever met. I am grateful for your friendship of almost 30 years.

To Adriana Wetzel, for being an angel in my life, providing emotional support, and showing me my true value and worth.

To Ivani Rezende, for bringing my work to life with such passion.

TABLE OF CONTENTS

Preface

The moment we open our eyes to who we really are, we are presented with a great opportunity. We can cleanse ourselves of what no longer fits. In this cleansing, we become more and more crystal clear, embracing a crystaline self, and the image and likeness of the One who creates us.

Have you ever noticed how our lives are filled with events that prompt us to rethink everything?

Whether or not we use these events for our learning and evolution depends on how willing we are to transform our journey. Sometimes, these significant events are not circumstances but people who make us see that there are different ways of being and even more effective ways of activating our potential.

Because we are social beings, we are not here to shut ourselves away in a bubble but to hold hands and help each other, especially in this socio-historical context marked by judgments, inequalities, and challenges.

Often, this context is overwhelming, leaving us confused, unsure of what to do, and even leading us to behaviors and choices that hinder our enthusiasm and overall well-being. That's why we have events and people in our lives, almost as if by divine synchronicity, who will always inspire and activate us so that we can overcome challenges and see the opportunities for evolution that we have in every moment.

Imagine, then, curious reader, when these forces to be reckoned with undergo this personal transformation and realize they can help and serve others with a profound sense of confidence by embracing them. If you haven't met someone like that yet, you will soon meet the force that is Cleo Pillon. She is a strong, authentic woman, a great mother who welcomes and helps, and a person who inspires everyone around her.

Today, she is a master of value-based connection, helping, welcoming, and developing people. From her history of deprivation to her current project, Salto Alto Connection (High Heel Connection), Cleo holds within her heart a dream with such purity of what she will always be: a strong and authentic woman.

Fueled by courage and faith, these dreams moved her along challenging paths rich in learning and self-development. Giving up is always an easy choice in life, but it is in overcoming it that we face the most difficult choice. During her journey, giving up was never one of the options Cleo chose in her heart.

That's precisely why Cleo's journey wasn't easy. The amount of learning and opportunities she had were divinely providential. But what good is all this if not to be shared, expanded, and used with love to help those around us more wisely?

There comes a time in our lives when we need to take pride in our actions and be less concerned with our possessions. Our actions cause our positive potential to ramify in this world and root our authentic being in this beautiful journey.

For you, dear reader, who are just starting to read this book, know that everything in our lives is a great opportunity for learning. From a conversation to a day at work or even from a personal object to an event in our daily lives.

The question is whether we are open-hearted enough to see all these opportunities, use them to expand our experiences, and become wiser individuals.

So, dear reader, may you continue reading with an open heart so that you can use this story of overcoming and success as a learning experience, an inspiration, and perhaps even an opportunity to build new, valuable connections that will help you on your wonderful and unique journey towards your full potential.

A book, a movie, or a work of art are individual creations until they are enjoyed by those who observe them. Every creation communicates something, shares something, generates impact, stimulates thought, and even transforms the journey of those who observe it.

Cleo shares an honest life experience in this creation, but she goes much further than that. She uses this experience to transform her story into an element of help. As she says, "Salto Alto (which could also be translated as Big Leap) is not about shoes. It's about our lives."

With this in mind, Cleo offers you, dear reader, the chance to look at this creation that begins here as an excellent opportunity to make your own choices, reach your potential, and live your life more authentically, with courage and faith. Only then will you be able to take ever-higher leaps on your journey toward personal success.

Igor Oak
Psychologist

Introduction

I've always had one certainty: my life experiences have a greater purpose. I knew that the entire process of getting here would lead me to a professional project that encourages others to understand that experiences can be transformative when we connect with our essence.

In this context, essence is not tied to a particular religion or belief. Its meaning is broader than that. We possess within us all the knowledge we need to address our issues. The problem is that this knowledge is not easy to access.

That's why we repeat our behaviors, as well as those of our parents, in an attempt to find ourselves again. We often suffer such deep pain that we don't see a light at the end of the tunnel. With all these feelings, we believe that if it has always been like this, why would it be any different now? We create a process of accepting our condition as an individual or family pattern.

Finding yourself is the greatest meaning of life. It is to understand why we are in this world, living with such different people and going through such diverse situations, which take us from one place to another in the blink of an eye.

By sharing my story, I aim to inspire those who are struggling and feel disconnected from achieving success. I also want to show that something greater drives our lives, making us move from our current state to project ourselves forward. A force that is a source of light.

The project I present in this book was born from my initial thoughts and reflections over time. It resulted from my experiences and learnings as I recognized myself and increasingly awakened my awareness of self-development.

Just as faith in myself and my potential to connect with divine creation, resilience, and my ability to overcome were internal tools constantly activated when I understood that the most significant force driving all the change I wanted to achieve came from my heart. Proactivity is one of the skills I've developed since I was a child, but the emotional issues were something I still had to work on.

At times, I heard that my hands were miraculous and that I could make people feel happier through them. This was gratifying but distressing because, in my heart, I still felt the pain of a child hurt by rejection and abandonment. I felt small in front of the world. Despite the incredible feedback, I didn't recognize my potential. This led to a lack of self-respect and constant defeats that required a lot of resignation and strength to get up again.

The toll of emotional, financial, and unresolved love relationships wore me down day after day. Once I realized the cure lay within me, I began moving upward in all areas of my life. I realized I wouldn't be loved if I didn't learn to love myself first. I wouldn't succeed as a professional if I didn't recognize my value. Everything would be diminished.

Thus, my brand and recognition as an entrepreneur in the cosmetics field were born from the skill of my hands and my love of self-care. Today, Aegisderma products are sold in Brazil, Europe, and the United States, bringing beauty, well-being, and self-esteem.

Because of my desire to be embraced, the Salto Alto Connection project was born. Based on three pillars presented throughout the book, this method is organized to balance emotional issues harmoniously and instrumentally while also boosting personal and professional life.

The Salto Alto Connection project has always existed within me. Still, I only realized it when I dared to face my shadows and admit they existed while redefining fear, guilt, and non-recognition. Only when I learned that we are just as we should be did I truly accept myself and find the strength to leave the place I had put myself in.

So, this book isn't about using fashion or accessories to camouflage your appearance. It's about truths, internal and external struggles, positioning, discoveries, and redefining. The high heel I am referring to here is not a style of shoe but an expression charged with overcoming life's adversities, with forgiveness in recognizing that we are part of a whole and the importance of each part in this chain of encounters with one's deepest self.

Each chapter of the book metaphorically represents the big leaps that this woman, born in the sertão (backlands), unnoticed by most, made to develop an authentic path, seeking opportunities to spread her best, activating the potential of other women in particular.

I, Cleo Pillon, with everything I've lived through and all the knowledge I've acquired through my experiences, am thrilled to bring to life this project that has been in my heart for a long time. Together, we can activate our positive potential and awaken the best within us to make great leaps by using tools that provide knowledge and connections. So...

Welcome to the *"Salto Alto Connection"* Program!

CHAPTER I

BAREFOOT: THE FIRST EMOTIONAL EXPERIENCES

The Barefoot Girl

I was born in northeast Brazil, on the Amazon, bathed by the *Tocantins* River and dirt roads that carry the stories of indigenous people and European Colonizers.

I was a small child with thin legs and arms, very dark hair, and skinny. My little heart was already beating with love for my father, Pedro, and my mother, Maria. The piece of land was the *Serra do Cravinho*, a group of mountains that surrounds the cities of *Imperatriz* and *João Lisboa* in *Maranhão*.

It is a simple place, home to humble people, with almost no information when you search the internet. *Serra do Cravinho* is one of those practically forgotten places in Brazil, where those who get there hope to own a piece of land to farm or produce *carnauba* (palm wax) and *babassu* (a type of palm tree).

I'm the third born of the children: Luísa, Keila, Cleudiana, Rui, Mel, Fernando, and Thais (we only share a mother with the last three siblings). And out of all of them, I was always the dreamer. The one who looked up at the sky and loved looking at the stars, imagining what was in the sky behind them. I believed that one day, I would go far. All I had to do was be brave.

"Go on, my child! Don't give up! Believe in yourself!" my father always told me. And this became my life motto: *Never give up.*

Our house was a wattle and daub hut; the beds were stretched-out hammocks, and the toys were little pieces of our imagination. The environment was very simple but full of care, especially from my maternal grandparents, Antônio and Raimunda, with whom we lived most.

Grandpa Antônio was my favorite. He used to take me to

the fields to plant beans or harvest corn. He looked after me, and since I was tiny, he loved putting me in one of the baskets on his donkey. On top of the straw, I could feel the wind on my face and the sun burning my skin. I loved being next to him because he did everything I wanted.

Grandma Raimunda, on the other hand, was beautiful at heart and very patient with me. She loved to make *pamonha* (a traditional Brazilian sweet corn dish) with the corn that Grandpa Antônio and I picked in the fields, and she taught me how to separate the best husks from the cobs to put the *pamonha* inside. Her hair was long and white, and I loved watching her brush it after the shower. The brush glided slowly so that all the strands were untangled.

There were legumes, vegetables, and fruit in the backyard of her house. I loved helping my grandmother harvest the produce that was ready to eat. I can still taste the beans and okra that Grandma Raimunda used to make with so much love.

On very hot days, she would take us to the river's edge near her house so my sisters and I could play in the water. It was one of the moments that I loved the most. My grandmother said those waters carried many of our ancestors' stories.

Another grandmother I treasure is my father's mother, Isabel, who was very affectionate with me. In the kitchen of her house, there was a wood-burning stove with a large burner and smaller ones around it. She'd have me sit on the extended part of the stove to watch her cook. I loved it when the rice sizzled slightly at the bottom of the pan because she would scoop it up with a spoon, roll it into a ball, and give it to me. I called the little balls of burnt rice "Captain."

There was a coconut tree in her backyard, from which little white worms, such as gongs or coconut bugs, emerged. She would take the worms and put them on the fire. Then, she would give them to me to eat. I don't remember what they tasted like. I just know I liked them because she said they would be good for me.

How I loved staying with my grandparents! Although I was very young, I still remember running barefoot on the dirt floor or feeling the cold water in the river.

Where Are You, Mom?

Since my father was a truck driver, he traveled a lot and spent much time away from home. He worked for a well-known company in the metropolitan region of southwest *Maranhão*. So when I turned four, he thought it best to move to the city of *Imperatriz*, which is close to the border with the state of *Tocantins*. This would make it easier for him to access the *Belém-Brasília* highway with the truck, and we would have the opportunity to study in larger schools, as the city was more economically developed.

Unlike the hut we lived in with my grandparents, our new house was made of bricks and had two bedrooms, a living room, a kitchen, and a bathroom. It was more spacious inside, with flooring throughout and a double bed. However, we still slept in hammocks.

My father bought us a television set so we wouldn't have to play outside the house. We watched cartoons like The Smurfs, Adventures of the Gummi Bears, and Dungeons & Dragons. Our entertainment also included superhero cartoons, such as Wonder Woman and Superman.

But what I liked most was hearing the horn of my father's truck as it approached the house. I would run to the window overlooking the street and wait for him to park that huge pink truck with the company sign sticking out. Sometimes, he'd let me sit in the driver's seat, and I would turn the steering wheel as if I were driving.

My father looked like one of those superheroes I used to see in cartoons when he got out of his truck. I thought about how strong he had to be to drive that giant truck and how brave he was. He told us about his adventures on the roads during his trips when facing storms, the darkness of the night, and the many dangers that always appeared. I loved my father very much, and I loved being close to him when he was at home, even if sometimes he got angry with us when we were up to no good.

When we moved to the city, my mother always stayed home. I carry many memories of my grandmother and grandfather, but I have no memories of my mother. But I knew she was always around.

During one of my father's trips, she left the house without telling us or saying goodbye. She packed her clothes and left without leaving a note or taking any of her children. And she stayed away for a long time.

I remember that morning, I woke up before my brothers and was surprised by the silence in the house. I looked in the living room, but she wasn't there. I went into the kitchen, and no one was there. There wasn't even breakfast on the table. I opened the kitchen door, and there was nothing.

My sisters woke up and found it strange that our mother wasn't home. We thought she was nearby and would be back soon. But time went by, and our hunger began to increase.

Then, my older sister picked up Rui, who was still small, and took us to the house of my father's sister, Aunt Concita, who lived nearby.

As my mother didn't come home that day, or the next, or even the day after, my aunt stayed at our house until my father returned from his trip. I didn't stand at the window waiting for him to arrive that day. My aunt asked us to stay indoors quietly so she could talk to my father outside.

As soon as he entered the house, an overwhelming sadness enveloped him as he pulled out a seat with his head hanging low, practically between his knees, weighed by the truth of it all. After a while, he called the four of us and said our mother wouldn't be coming home anymore. He would leave us at Grandmother Isabel's house until he had sorted out everything he needed.

He didn't explain anything else or give us the right to ask questions. It was as simple as that. My mother wasn't coming back. My aunt fell silent and said nothing more. Everyone fell silent, and no one dared to say her name. I held onto that sadness in my childish heart without shedding a tear.

We were split between the houses of my Grandmother Isabel and my aunt. My aunt Luzinete, my mother's sister, also took turns with Aunt Concita to look after me and my siblings. In addition to them, our neighbor Altair always took care of us.

She became even more attached to me because she didn't have a daughter, only sons. I was her baby. She always gave me new dresses and loved to comb my hair. She loved me so much that she even asked my father to adopt me. But he didn't accept it and said he would not separate the children. He also said she should marry him if she wanted to keep me.

A Mother At Heart

My father remarried almost a year after my mother left. After the wedding, we moved in with Altair, who became our new mother. This gave me two brothers: Gerson, who was my sister Luísa's age, and Gledson, who was two years younger than me.

I was always very fond of Altair, and we became even closer after she married my father. I was five years old when they married. I have many memories of that time, mainly because I gained another set of grandparents.

Altair's parents became my godparents when I was baptized in the Orthodox Church. I loved spending vacations at my grandfather's house (I began to call him that) in a countryside neighborhood called Taboquinha. There, I helped him by trampling rice, drawing water from the well and carrying it like a can on my head, and washing clothes in the river with soap that my grandmother made.

Life on the farm was very simple, yet I felt very comfortable at my grandparents' house. When I stayed there in the afternoons, Altair would accompany me to the river so I could bathe and play diving games with the other children.

Because her family was huge, she had many nephews. It was always a real party. The older ones could climb the bridge that crossed the river and jump into the deepest part. The younger ones just watched and imagined that, as soon as they got older, they would do the same.

Since my father was prone to anger and Altair didn't want to contradict him, we weren't allowed to play outside, especially after six in the evening. So, our lives were limited to playing inside and helping her with the chores. I took advantage of the school vacations to have fun because I knew I couldn't play with other children when I returned to the city.

I studied in the afternoon, and my sisters in the morning. While they were at school, I helped Altair by doing my chores at home. Then, I showered, ate lunch, and went to school. In the afternoon, my sisters took care of their chores.

The chores were divided between the three sisters. The boys didn't help, and Rui was still small. Our chores consisted of washing the bathroom, cleaning up the dog's poop, cleaning the backyard, dusting the furniture, cooking, and sweeping the house. At the same time, Altair stayed in the sewing room, working on customer orders.

As an excellent seamstress, she had many customers and worked all day. As a result, she relied on our daily help to look after the house and the food. She was very attentive to us and worried about us, too. Even so, we missed our biological mother very much. Altair couldn't make up for it, no matter how hard she tried.

As the eldest, at 10 years old, Luísa looked after her younger siblings with help from Keila, who was 8. However, ever since my biological mother left, Keila became very rebellious. That's why, as a teenager, she decided to live with Grandmother Raimunda so she wouldn't constantly argue with Altair.

I was very sad when Keila left home because she left me just like my mother. Even as a child, I wondered what I had done wrong for my mother to go and not take me with her.

Whenever I asked about my mother at my grandparents' house, no one could explain what had happened to her, and I felt sad about it. In my young heart, I believed she would return any moment, and I was always left waiting.

Mom, Are You Back?

After being away for almost two years, I saw my mother standing outside the gate on my way out of school one evening. I could hardly believe what I was seeing, so I ran towards her, hugging her tightly. She had come home.

My older sister was also waiting for me at the school gate. Altair took me to school, and my sister accompanied me back home daily. But that day, she stayed away. She didn't come near me.

I just sat there clutching my mother's legs, telling her how much I missed her and that I was sure she would come back for me one day. She hugged me back and said she missed me, too. She said she had left hoping to give all her children a better life and would come back to see me more often. My mother asked me not to be sad or angry with her, like my sisters were. She said that one day, I would understand everything she had done.

Even though I looked at my sister several times, she didn't return my gaze. I don't think Luísa could handle the situation. She was furious and didn't even want to look at our mother's face. That's why she remained distant, just waiting for me to decide to let go of her and leave.

I was still too young to understand the real reasons for my mother's absence and couldn't go home alone. So, I had to say goodbye to her before heading towards my sister, who was already impatient with my delay. I kept looking back several times and waving to my mother while she went the other way.

I went home very happy that day. I knew she hadn't forgotten me. I knew she loved me. Despite what people had told me—even the kids at school—I had a mother. And now she wasn't just a figment of my imagination. I touched her and felt her embrace.

I was so happy that I ran to Altair as soon as I got home and told her what had happened. She became serious as if trying to understand what I was saying. She came to her senses only after my older sister confirmed my story. At that moment, I realized how much she loved me. Her reaction was one of despair at the possibility of losing the daughter she loved so much.

After my mother's return, Luísa also decided to leave home. That day, I felt even sadder because I felt cast aside by both my sisters and my biological mother. I realized I had to be my own foundation and couldn't count on anyone.

I already missed Keila, and now Luísa's departure made me sadder. Mixed feelings took over me. The desire to remain in my childhood and the desire to grow up were in conflict within my chest, as if I were about to explode at any moment. I was no longer a child, and the changes in my body showed that.

I didn't know these sensations, much less how to deal with them. If the pain was intense in childhood, imagine adolescence and the turmoil of feelings that erupt during this phase! I wanted to be free, but I still had no idea what this freedom that my sisters questioned or that I wanted meant.

With no one to talk to, feelings of sadness, rejection, loneliness, and abandonment surrounded my thoughts. I ended up losing myself, idealizing a reality that could never exist. I suffered silently, creating a perfect world where everything was possible. A place where nothing from my living reality could ever reach.

The Little Box Of Emotions

The sadness I felt at the absence of my sisters was excruciating. It's too complicated for a child to deal with feelings they don't yet have the neurological training to understand. I was only 4 years old when my mother left. Imagine the sense of abandonment and the pain of the absence of a motherly figure.

My sister's reaction also affected me. Luísa suffered in silence, trying to help us deal with the situation in the best way possible by taking on a role that wasn't hers and shouldn't belong to a child. Keila reacted with rebellion to the feelings that didn't fit in her heart.

I kept quiet in my childish world, trying to hold onto the memories of my mother that seemed to fade with the days. The memories of my grandmothers and aunts were clear, but that of my motherly figure threatened to slip away.

So, to keep the memories inside my heart, I created a visualization to keep them alive. Like those little music boxes I used to see in soap operas and were enchanted by the melody they played, I learned to keep my feelings in figurative boxes.

From my childish perspective, this was the only way to protect myself from what bothered me and from answers I didn't have to the questions I could barely formulate. I could only feel it, and because it hurt, I kept it hidden so I wouldn't stare at it all the time. So, despite being emotional, I learned not to show my emotions so much, including crying.

I had no idea what holding onto my feelings would do to me in the future, and even if I had, I didn't have the resources to do anything different—not at that age, not without someone who could help me endure all those situations that weren't mine but hurt me so much.

Ever since my mother left home, I had closed my heart and ears even tighter still so as not to hear what was being said. Like the superhero cartoons I watched, I wanted super strength to fight the persistent enemy that made me sad. However, it was large and would scare me when I was alone or woke up suddenly in the middle of the night.

In those moments, I'd cover my head to hide myself. And I remembered what people said: "When you grow up, little girl, all this will pass." So, I wanted to grow up soon to chase away the fear of feeling alone in the darkroom or of the hauntings that the elders told in stories to scare us.

Even if I begged, I knew that no one would come to my rescue from those monsters. So I kept quiet with my little boxes of what I felt so that no one would realize they were stored away. If one of them found out, they would move them, and that sadness could return at any moment.

As a child without any psychological or emotional support, I had no idea of the traumas that parental abandonment would bring into my life. I now know early childhood experiences are the most important for healthy development. And a sequence of negative experiences during this period can trigger mental disorders in other stages of life.

Traumas formed in childhood can influence behavior, thoughts, beliefs, emotion management, relationships, and even adult achievements. According to the British psychoanalyst John Bowlby (1907-1990), the creator of attachment theory, the absence of maternal or paternal care leads to sadness, anger, and anguish.

During early childhood, the minor details in the relationship between a baby and its parents, especially the mother as the primary caregiver, can interfere with development. The child deeply feels the quality of the touch, gaze, speech, and closeness between parents and children.

Children cannot yet understand the emotions resulting from actions and words in all their nuances, so they feel intensely. Their misinterpretations guide them throughout their growth into adulthood.

When parental abandonment occurs, the child cannot understand the parent's intentions or feelings toward them. As a result, the child experiences various negative emotions, which become part of their being, both consciously and unconsciously.

I felt all of this. So, I got used to not establishing emotional ties with others because I could lose them at any moment. How could I connect to others with love if I didn't receive love?

At the beginning of my adolescence, I struggled to establish my identity and place in the world, so I hid from myself and others. I thought I was a bad person and no one would ever truly like or care for me.

Even with Altair present, I didn't get the affection I expected. She lived with her own traumas, so expressing affection through gestures wasn't easy for her. However, she never stopped looking after me and pleasing me with the resources she had at her disposal.

With all that I was feeling, the desire to break free and follow the path of the stars towards fulfilling my dreams was growing in my heart. I just didn't know how that would happen.

CHAPTER 2

A Small Leap: Self-Affirmation In Adolescence

The Girl Woman

When my sisters left, I started to feel very lonely and wondered what it would be like if I moved in with my mother, too. Now, there was no one to share the daily chores with. And that made me very angry because there was no time left to play or laze around.

I remember that Altair's living room had a piece of pink ceramic and various porcelain animals on the bookshelf that she liked collecting. I was very jealous of her collection, and she always asked me to clean it very carefully so as not to break any of it. As it took a long time to clean, and I was afraid of dropping them, I found it a very dull task.

Because I was no longer a child, I also took over the cooking. From time to time, she taught me how to make pastries and ice cream to sell around the neighborhood to earn a little extra money. But I ate almost all the goods. Even so, I could make enough money to pay for the ingredients and not leave her at a loss.

She wanted to prepare me for life in case I decided to leave home, too. And that was a real possibility for her. That's why she taught me to do all the housework, cook, and even run a small business. She saw in me a proactivity that I hadn't realized I had.

Whenever I had free time, I would watch television and imagine being inside that little box one day as a famous TV host. I would playfully take a corncob, pretend it was a microphone, and talk to my audience, mostly my brother Rui. I would interview objects as if they were people and thank them for the successful program I had.

Like the TV hosts, I dreamed of having long, straight hair. But Altair didn't let me grow it out. She said that short hair was more practical to upkeep and easier to avoid lice. So, one day, a school friend and I bought a paste to straighten my hair. Even though it was very smelly, we applied the mixture. I was thrilled with the result! I finally had the hair I'd always dreamed of.

But Altair wasn't happy when she saw me with my hair straightened and smelly. She got very angry, took me by the arm, and made me sit on a stool. She grabbed scissors and cut the strands close to my scalp to remove all the straightening. I've never had my hair so short. I've also never cried so much in my life. My dream was spreading across the floor in dark strands cut by her.

I realized that from that day on, something inside me had changed. Altair had disrespected me, and she had no right to do that. She wasn't my biological mother. A huge disappointment permeated my heart, and I felt rejected yet again.

She didn't like me as much as she said she claimed. My anger grew even more the next day when I arrived at school with very short hair. The laughter of my classmates echoed in my head for the rest of the day.

Whenever she realized she had crossed the line, she would try to do something to make me happy and forgive her. That day, I was gifted a new dress. She asked me not to be angry with her and that she only wanted to protect me. She also said that my hair was too beautiful to straighten, and I shouldn't use those strong products because they could harm me and were very smelly.

Deep down, I thought she was jealous and perhaps felt that she was losing me. In any case, I couldn't stay angry with Altair for long. I knew that she worked a lot and only thought about my well-being.

At the end of the afternoon, she would close the sewing room and sit on a green macaroni chair in the living room. In those moments, I would take the brush and start combing her hair. I would then put a cream called Rose Milk on my hands and massage it into her face. Eventually, she fell asleep, and I was happy to see her resting.

In one of those moments, as soon as she woke up, she hugged me and said:

"Daughter, your hands are healing! When you grow up, you'll be able to care for people's beauty and well-being."

I didn't understand what she meant then, but I knew my destiny lay in her words.

Taking care of Altair was the greatest form of affection I could have in return for what she did for me. But our relationship as mother and daughter was changing. We did the same things together, but we no longer had that bond of love that we had when I was a child.

She sensed that I would soon be leaving home. And so little by little, she was letting go of her beloved *daughter*. I still loved my *mother at heart*, but something stronger in my chest told me that I had to go to my biological mother and my sisters.

Determined Or Rebellious?

Since Gledson was two years younger than me, he did everything he could to tease me, especially when he became a teenager. I confess that he was very annoying sometimes, and I would lose my temper and slap him. However, after getting very annoyed on one of those mornings, I grabbed his neck and scratched him with all my strength.

Hearing her son's screams, Altair left her room and headed

for the living room. As soon as she arrived and saw her son's neck all scratched, she turned around and slapped me across the face. I didn't react at the time. All I could do was place my hand on my cheek as a stinging pain made the impact grow hot. Then I ran out with tears streaming from my eyes. The slap didn't just hurt my face. It hurt my heart. I would never have imagined being beaten by Altair.

That day, I was silent and devastated. Something inside my heart had broken. I took a shower and went to school. On the way, I thought about everything I felt and the slap I had received. I missed my biological mother and my sisters terribly. So after school, I took the road in the opposite direction and walked for almost two hours until I reached their house.

My sisters were surprised by my arrival and told me my mother was traveling that day. I cried a lot and told them everything that had happened.

When I didn't come home that day, Altair was very worried. At school, they told her that I had gone out alone. She knew I was upset and assumed I had gone to my mother's house, so she asked acquaintances if I was there.

When I left school the next day, she waited for me and asked me to come home. She said she'd been frustrated but didn't want me to push her away. I insisted, saying that the slap had hurt a lot and that I didn't want to go back.

She persisted, saying that my father was coming home from a trip and would be very angry with me. I continued defying her and told her to tell him I was living with my mother. I knew my father would be very angry with her for letting me leave home and live with my mother. Unconsciously, it was my way of getting back at her for what she had done.

I can't explain what happened that day. I was revolted by the whole situation, especially the slap I received. I was growing up and no longer the innocent girl everyone knew. In a way, I was imposing my will and demanding my freedom, just as my sisters did.

I left Altair alone at the school gate and returned to my mother's house. That afternoon, I went to my father's house with my sisters to get my clothes and everything I owned. Her sadness at seeing me put my clothes in little bags was heartbreaking, but I didn't let it get to me. I was determined to move.

When my father returned from his trip and didn't see me, he was furious and immediately went to my mother's house. He asked me to get my things and follow him. Reluctantly, I replied that I wasn't going back to his house. He could punish me if he wanted, but I still wouldn't give in. He was furious with my attitude and almost hit me then and there. I told him that he had also abandoned me. All he did was travel; I was tired of being stuck at home, yearning for my freedom.

After my father heard everything I'd said, he became very upset and decided to leave. I don't know if it was so he wouldn't hit me or because he felt guilty for everything that was happening in our lives. I felt good then, but after the fact, I felt a mixture of emotions inside my heart. After all, I loved my father very much and didn't want to hurt him.

Hello, Freedom!

Unlike my father's house, my mother's was simpler. The doors and windows did not close properly. The bathroom was outside, but there was no shower. I often felt terrified, especially when

I was alone. My sisters used to go out to meet their friends, and I stayed inside. Other than the rats that used to scare me from time to time by running around the house, there were also the men who raped the women. They were known as "perverts".

Like Altair, my mother always told us that if we saw a man in the yard, we should hide and stay put or run out to ask for help because they were usually armed with a pocketknife. If the woman resisted, he wouldn't hesitate to kill her.

As soon as it got dark, we tried not to stay in the yard or outside the house for fear of being caught off guard. The lack of safety was our biggest fear at my mother's house. Because we had to bathe with a hose, we had to do everything during the day or always be accompanied so that we could keep an eye on one another. This was also the case with our physiological needs.

Luckily, a neighbor watched the street at night and always tried to sit in front of my house when he realized I would be alone. It was the only way I could sleep a little more peacefully. Even so, I would get tense and take a long time to fall asleep, especially when I heard any noise, no matter how small. During the night, the rats would come out of their hiding places in search of food and wake me up anytime they dropped something.

I've often thought about returning to my father's house because I'd have more comfort, food, a shower, and a warm bed there. But I would think about it and remember how rigorous my education had been and how much I'd been asked to do, and that made me choose to pay the price of living that longed for freedom.

Over time, I got used to that way of life. My mother worked as a cook and spent days away from home on the farms that hired her. My sisters earned very little, barely enough to cover their expenses. So, I started devising strategies to earn extra money, like selling magazine catalogs or doing domestic work in the homes of people with better financial conditions.

The street my mother lived on had many good well kept houses. However, my mother's house was simple and not as grand, making the residents feel as if it was a soresight that would impoverish the area. To give you an idea, even a doctor's family lived there. That's why I always tried to be nice and gave the other girls whatever I had just to be friends with them and be invited to their homes to eat treats we couldn't afford.

On the other hand, I did small household chores in exchange for a plate of food. One of the neighbors liked to tell stories about the farm where she worked, and she always brought back the bird skins so we could make fried rice. I would wait for her to come home from work and rush to help her with the housework. Afterward, we would have dinner together.

Another neighbor who liked me very much had a bakery at the back of her house. I used to go there around lunchtime and offer to help with the housework to earn bread or cassava cake.

When I turned 13, I got a job at a shoe store in town. Child labor was allowed at the time, so I was hired on a small salary. I sold shoes and cleaned the store.

Because I was very young and because of the dangers of the area, the owner and his wife wouldn't let me go out for lunch. So she'd bring food for the three of us, almost always rice, beans, and eggs. I can still taste the flavors in my mouth today. They were both very good to me.

To compensate for the affection, I helped a lot in the store. I've always been proactive, so I wasn't shy about doing things and tried to get things done before I was asked. I worked in the store for a year. After that, the owner couldn't keep my salary because his wife got sick.

I needed to help with the rent, so I returned to selling catalogs or any other product offered. Unfortunately, because of my naivety, I was often scammed and didn't get paid. At other times, I was so distracted by the sales that I lost track of time and missed school. Due to situations like that, I failed a few grades in school and fell behind my classmates. I always liked studying, but coping with everything I was going through was hard.

Goodbye, Imperatriz!

My sister Keila got married very young, and the relationship didn't work out, so she decided to move to São Paulo with her baby daughter and her sister-in-law. She craved other opportunities far from *Imperatriz*.

Even with the promise that she would take me to live with her as soon as she settled in the new city, the feeling of abandonment took hold of my heart again. Every time I witnessed a departure, the sadness intensified. I felt like I was becoming invisible in the face of these circumstances and the people I loved.

So that I wouldn't be alone, my mother rented a cafe near our house, and I started helping her with the menus and cleaning the place. We started spending more time together and getting to know each other better, even though we had disagreements from time to time.

Although we got closer, our relationship remained challenging. When I moved in with my biological mother, I was around 11 years old. At the time, she spent much time on the farms where she worked. When she returned, she would purchase many things at the market to please her daughters, including goodies we liked and didn't have daily.

She was also an excellent cook, always preparing tasty food for us to eat together. These moments were perfect because I felt part of the family. The warm welcome gave me the feeling of belonging.

When she rented out the cafe, she divided the house into small rooms so that each of us could have one, and she could rent out the others to help with the finances. Each room had a stove, a gas cylinder, a small table, and a bed. The fridge was communal, and the bathroom remained outside.

In a way, this separation reinforced my feelings of rejection. It was strange to be in the same space but not together. This only intensified my rebelliousness to attract my mother's attention. Deep down, I needed to be seen by her. I didn't know how to express my feelings, and she didn't understand my needs.

At the time, I understood that behaving affrontively was a way of seeking maternal love. I couldn't do anything differently, but neither could she. Then came the fights, the disobedience, the insults that tried to expose the pain that I felt and that was trapped in my heart.

She punished me by grounding me, and I punished her with rebellion. In this duel, we hurt ourselves and each other. It's hard for a teenager to deal with feelings while controlling impulsivity and anger. Afterward, there is a kind of regret, but the reaction is inevitable, however painful it may be.

In a way, leaving *Imperatriz* and living with my sister was the only way I could escape my feelings. I hoped that if I left the city, everything would be okay. Especially when, between one story and another, she said that the capital of São Paulo was very different, and I would have more opportunities for work and to be someone in life. That fed my heart and soul.

I knew I didn't belong in that city or with those people. I knew that one day, I would be far away and recognized for my talent. In fact, due to my sensitivity, intuition has been part of my life since I was a little girl. The revelations came in dreams, sudden episodes, or words that I didn't quite know how they appeared, and surprised even Altair. And this time, my intuition told me that I should go. And so, I did.

About a year after Keila had left, in one of our phone calls, she asked me to move to São Paulo as soon as I could. She needed someone to share a house with her and her young daughter. At that moment, the opportunity I had wanted so much materialized.

To raise money for the trip, I sold everything I had, including a stove and a used gas cylinder that were a part of my room. At the time, I got around $100, enough for the one-way ticket and the installment to contribute to the rent of the place where my sister would be moving with her daughter.

As the journey was long and I couldn't spend much on food, I made a chicken *farofa* (fried yucca flour) to take with me as a packed lunch. Alongside my few clothes, I packed my faith, courage, and many dreams in a small suitcase.

When I left, I confess that the hardest part was not saying goodbye to Altair or my father; instead, it was not saying goodbye to my younger brothers, who were with Grandmother Raimunda. Since my mother was no longer running the cafe, I was unable to say goodbye to her because she was now working out of town.

Fernando, who was most attached to me, cried the most. Seeing those little eyes full of tears hurt my heart, but I had to be strong and follow my destiny. So, I kissed him and promised that I would return for him one day.

With an aching heart but confidence in this new step, I got on the bus to São Paulo. Through the window of the moving vehicle, I said goodbye to my childhood and adolescence, taking only the story I had lived during those seventeen years.

An Image In The Mirror

As I grew up, I began to value my appearance more and more, especially because living with my sisters and my mothers encouraged that. I also saw lotions, perfumes, and make-up in the catalogs I sold to my clients.

How it all dazzled me! I wanted to be like the girls in the magazines with their beautiful skin, perfect makeup, and shiny straight hair. It was my dream to have all of that.

I decided to keep my feelings in little boxes and locked them away in my heart so they couldn't be accessed. It was my way of coping with the fear I felt on nights when I was alone, of the stories of the evil men who ruined the dreams of girls like me.

Even though I was no longer a child and had learned to deal with many situations, I still felt small in the face of the world and everything I didn't know. I really admired my mother because she had the courage to leave home and see a world she hadn't known until then. But I was afraid and felt alone.

Sometimes, I even asked my mother why she left home when I was a child. The answer: I wasn't yet old enough to understand everything she had experienced in her relationship with my father and why she had left everything behind to find her way and live the life she wanted.

I wasn't sure I wanted to know about my mother's life. I harbored many bad feelings and even judgments, which I thought, no matter how much she explained, I wouldn't understand at that moment. So, I preferred to stay silent, trapped in my world, accepting the conditions given to me.

I couldn't grasp the consequences of my lack of affection at the time. However, I could already see it in my attitude in many situations I've described. One was the need to satisfy people, putting them first, even at the risk of harming my basic needs. Sometimes, to have a friend, I would be willing to offer them the only plate of food I had.

I also subjected myself to household chores in exchange for affection, which was represented by a piece of cake, a plate of food, or the right to sit next to someone and talk to them. The feeling of inferiority was built into my life.

These situations exemplified how I experienced, expressed, and processed my feelings. In The Unconscious, Freud (1856-1939) defines affection as follows: "Affects and feelings correspond to processes of discharge, the final manifestations of which are perceived as sensations."

I didn't know the difference between emotion and feeling then, but I hardly expressed myself emotionally anymore. Because they are a neural response to external stimuli, emotions are instinctive, like crying and laughing. They give rise to feelings, the way we feel about an emotion, which is a more internalized process.

Only later did I understand that the little boxes of emotions I had imagined were feelings. According to Freud's theories, the **drawers of the unconscious** are "a kind of allegory which serves to illustrate a certain insight, to follow the numerous narcissistic smells which ascend from each of our drawers." Feelings are also individual. They belong to each person and change as they go through new experiences or come to know themselves in the face of the healing process.

The bus jolting along the way often woke me up from the sleep that came and took me out of the world of dreams, bringing me back to a reality that I still had no idea what it looked like, what I would encounter, and how I would survive.

Even so, I had faith because I knew that God would lead me down a new path and that I would have the opportunity to achieve everything that I hadn't had access to until that point. From then on, I dreamed, imagined, and planned my life.

And so it went on for the two and a half days of traveling along roads and places I had no idea existed. The world was opening up before my eyes, and a new life was unfolding.

I took the small mirror in my bag and fixed my hair to get out to my next destination.

CHAPTER 3

THE FIRST LEAP:
FROM IMPERATRIZ
TO SÃO PAULO

Next Stop: São Paulo

As soon as I disembarked at the Tietê bus station, I was amazed at the number of people moving from one place to another, and the noise of the bus engines pulling up on the platforms. I barely knew how to get around the disembarkation area. As soon as I spotted my sister, my heart filled with joy.

She lived in *Jardim Dracena*, on the city's west side, so she asked her ex-sister-in-law to help her pick me up from the bus station so she wouldn't get lost on the bus routes. The journey by car took about an hour.

Along the way, I was amazed at the size of the city. Everything was new to a girl who had just arrived in São Paulo, from the gray sky to the barely breathable air. It was as if I were on another planet, engulfed by an unknown mist, and not knowing what was ahead.

Since my sister arrived in the city, she had been living with her ex-sister-in-law, so she had no furniture. The house she had rented was in the same area where she lived, on the private side of the neighborhood. It had three rooms and a bathroom inside. To help us, her ex-sister-in-law offered us a stove, a gas cylinder, and a mattress.

The rent for the space amounted to something like $500 today. My sister was unemployed, had a child, and had only $250 to pay the rent and buy what she needed to support herself.

I had only $100 to pay the first month's rent. I had nothing else. My situation was extremely precarious, to say the least. Even so, my arrival made my sister more hopeful.

Intending to help us get furniture, the ex-sister-in-law asked me to accompany her to a store the next day to buy some on a credit system, with her as guarantor. As the installments would be paid monthly, I would look for a job as soon as we left the store as a guarantee for the purchase.

I confess that this moment was not what I expected. I came from a completely different reality from a big city. I was very shy and had a strong *Maranhão* accent, and I could hear people's mocking laughter. I was unemployed and had nothing to offer except my character.

The conversation with the salesman wasn't very straightforward. He didn't want to sell me the furniture despite my promise to pay on time. The fact that I was unemployed made it challenging to negotiate. After much insistence, he called the manager, and I bought a closet, two beds, a mattress, a kitchen table, and some pans.

It was my first achievement. Now, all I had to do was get a job, which took a lot of persistence. After a week, I got a job as a receptionist in a simple neighborhood hotel. To clock in at 6 a.m. I had to get up at 4 a.m. to make my lunch and have enough time for the bus ride. But I wasn't complaining, I was happy with my new reality.

In *Maranhão*, the weather is hot all year round. In São Paulo, I encountered soul-freezing cold weather, drizzle, and an icy wind that cut through my skin. Even so, I didn't shy away from a cold shower at dawn.

I was very inexperienced and naive, which caused me to be deceived by hotel guests who left without paying the room rates. As it was a small and simple place, people used it in bad faith and didn't pay their bills. Faced with this reality, the manager fired me because of the financial loss.

I was desperate because I couldn't lose my job. So I begged

her to let me stay, stating that I'd be willing to do any job in exchange for a salary. I explained that my sister and niece depended on me.

At my insistence, the manager gave in and offered me a job as a maid with a lower salary. As a maid, I was in charge of maintaining the cleanliness of each room and the entirety of the hotel. I washed bathrooms, did laundry, changed the sheets, and kept everything in order.

I was initially very sad about the new job, but I had no choice but to take it. I thanked God and the manager for the opportunity to continue working.

With my salary cut, I had to review my spending to pay the installments for the furniture while still having enough left over for the rent. But I was sure in my heart that an opportunity would come when I least expected it, I would get a better job and other opportunities that would enable me to afford all my needs. I kept my faith in God and my potential.

I worked at the hotel for six months and managed to cover the cost of the furniture and part of the rent. My sister did sporadic jobs for extra income, as she still had a very young daughter.

While working during the day, I started taking supplementary courses at a public school in the evening to complete my secondary education in a year and a half. I knew that to get a good opportunity, I needed to study and improve myself. I intended to take a technical or college course to become an esthetician. I was very grateful to the hotel's owner for letting me stay as a maid, but I wouldn't have had many opportunities there.

If It Hadn't Been For That Liquor...

Then, an opportunity came to me. A friend referred me to a potential position at a multinational company that manufactures juices and other drinks. Following the guidelines he gave me, I applied for the job. I put on my nicest clothes and prepared myself as best I could. I was a simple girl from the interior of *Maranhão* who might not stand a chance against the competition, but I couldn't be discouraged at the first hurdle. After all, I had talent, even if I didn't know what it was yet.

With the address in hand and hope in my heart, I headed down one of the main avenues in São Paulo's capital, *Faria Lima*. Known for its mirrored business buildings, it felt like a whole other world—something I'd only seen in soap operas. The company building was just as beautiful, and the office was on the tenth floor. I was heading for the top.

The interview was with the company's director. The proposal was to advertise a liquor launch to the public market. Eight girls were considered for the role of promoter. I remained confident and attentive to everything that was being explained.

The interview dynamic involved selling an egg yolk-based liquor, which, despite its strange composition, was very fragrant and tasty. This was my chance to share my talent. I unconsciously raised my hand and asked to be the first to perform the test. In front of the director's gaze and the other candidates, I offered a product I had never tried before, and my boldness marked the start of my career.

The director heard what I was saying and sounded surprised as he said he would buy the liquor because my friendliness and words had won him over. The first big door in my professional career opened right then and there.

The meager salary was now expanding abundantly and included excellent benefits I would have as an employee of the company. My life improved significantly, and my sister's did too. We managed to leave the house we were living in and move to another location with better leisure and logistical conditions.

As a product promoter, I visited several supermarkets in different parts of the city. That's why the new location would be more beneficial to my commute. I started to get to know São Paulo. I traveled throughout the city center and areas in the north, south, east, and west, carrying the company's products. It was the first time I felt fulfilled. I was experiencing my first big leap since arriving in São Paulo.

However, I still had a lot to learn.

"Who are you again?"
"Cleudiana."
"Difficult name, different accent."
"Where are you from?"
"Imperatriz, in *Maranhão*."

This questioning strengthened my sense of inferiority because I valued what others thought about me, not who I was. If you don't learn to appreciate your own history and essence, comparison will rattle your feelings. I felt invisible standing before other stories, thinking my own didn't matter.

The fact that I was the daughter of a truck driver, my mother had abandoned me when I was still a child, having a lot of siblings, and having come from a place far away from the big Brazilian capitals, diminished me as a person, and this distanced me from my desires. To reach the top, to be known and recognized, and to be surrounded by important and successful people.

The problem is that when childhood scars are not healed, they start to find ways of compensating. My shortcomings and lack of guidance led me to lose my way financially.

I believed that if I looked good on the outside, wore nice clothes, perfect makeup, and the highest heels, I'd be complete. People would respect my appearance. Looks are undoubtedly very important, but that's not all that matters. What really counts is your essence, which I was losing.

At the time, I didn't consider the possibility of going to therapy. I tried to solve my internal issues as I thought they should be solved. However, facing the shadows that wander around in our unconscious is difficult. I entered a phase of constantly creating shortcuts and losing myself in the process.

The awe of my first salary at the multinational reinforced my idea of power. For someone who received less than the minimum wage as a maid at a small hotel, the pay as a product promoter wasn't that high, but it impressed me. Not to mention the dazzling world I felt like I had just entered. Senior executives with beautiful cars carried themselves as winners as they wore expensive and impressive clothes. I wanted it all.

I observed how the company's female executives dressed, did their hair, spoke, and behaved. It was an inspiration. I wanted to be like them. So I spent a lot on clothes, shoes, jewelry, handbags, and trips to the beauty salon.

After working for a while, I had no financial savings and had to work even harder. When I finished school, I managed to get my driver's license. My dream was to buy a Volkswagen Gol, the sensation at the time in Brazil. I loved the model, but it was expensive, so I couldn't make that dream come true.

Even so, an inner voice invited me to reconnect with something I had abandoned. I remembered Altair's words telling me I had magic hands and could help people feel good and happy. It was just a voice echoing in a reality I could not yet embrace. My career in the company was very important, so that's what I focused on.

I did my best in every establishment I worked at. I wanted to stand out, receive praise, and be applauded for my efficiency. That's why I always kept myself impeccable, not only in appearance but also by monitoring my speech and tone of voice to convey authority.

I was always on the lookout for company launches and tried to keep up with what was new on the market. I knew knowledge was also a way to stand out, so I strived for it.

However, fate had other plans. I had little idea of what was to come and how my life would change for the better. I was just a few steps away from living another story.

Almost Happily Ever After

I didn't have many romantic experiences in *Imperatriz*. When I arrived in São Paulo, my life was so busy that I barely had time to go out, have fun, or date.

However, I became very good friends with the executive director at one of the outlets where I worked. He had been divorced for a while and I think he fell in love with me because he was always talking to me and being nice. Since he was older, I greatly respected him and liked his kindness toward me.

During one of our conversations, he mentioned that he had a house on the coast of São Paulo and invited me to spend a weekend at the beach. I accepted the invitation but asked if I could bring a friend along. He smiled and said he'd invite a friend too. That's how I met my first husband.

That weekend, my friend ended up getting close to the executive director, and I to his friend. He was ten years older than me and worked at a transport company. We fell in love on our first date, so much so that we returned to the capital already dating.

It was imperative to have love by my side. It was only at that moment that I realized how much I needed a companion who loved me and made me feel safe next to someone who, in a way, protected me and took care of me. Our relationship grew gradually stronger, allowing us to spend many years together.

After a while of dating, one of his ways of caring for me was offering me an apartment in *Morumbi*. That way, I'd be closer to the city center, making it easier to get from one place to another and make my sales.

Later, he surprised me with a car to help me get around easily. Imagine my joy seeing that present in the garage! With the freedom to move around in the city, new door opened and I received a promotion in the company.

I became a promoter, the highest position in the area, with the right to promote the company's best products in large nightclubs, restaurants, steakhouses, and high-class events. Now that I had more time to do the routes, I could get home earlier and devote myself to my personal projects.

A few months later, I crashed my car, which resulted in a total loss, injuring my chin and head. As my job required me to be physically present in the stores, I resigned from the company I was working for.

With the money from my severance pay, I began to invest in

a dream that I had put aside since arriving in São Paulo. Now, feeling more secure and with my fiancé's support, I decided to pursue what I loved so much: esthetics.

I signed up for free courses in the area to learn how to do procedures such as facial cleansing, lymphatic drainage, and other specialties. Also, taking advantage of my free time, I asked an esthetician friend if I could sit in and observe the procedures at her clinic.

She noticed my skills and advised me to create my own space to offer my services. That advice warmed my heart with the certainty that my path in cosmetology was part of my trajectory.

I Now Pronounce You Husband And Wife

After three years of dating, my fiancé asked me to marry him. What a happy day that was! One of my dreams was coming true. My greatest wish was to have a family, a house, and children. I wanted to have the opportunity to tell a different story than my parents.

I wanted to love and be loved by whoever was by my side. My desire to be happy drove me to move forward and build a home anchored by faith and companionship, a home filled with love and respect.

So, with a beautiful party, a stunning wedding dress, and the honeymoon of my dreams, my fiancé and I exchanged rings.

Little by little, my life began to take on new contours of fulfillment, and everything moved towards achieving my dreams. I felt happy at that moment because I had someone who loved me by my side, a home, and a positive pregnancy test. That's right! I was pregnant.

The joy of having a child enveloped my heart during the first few months, but our idealized path is not always the same as the Creator's. Still in gestation, my little angel took flight and returned to the Father. At that moment, the sadness at my baby's departure also brought feelings of inadequacy and guilt.

"Do I not have the right to be a mother?" I asked myself amidst the pain of recovering from so many other moments up to that point. I deemed myself incapable in the face of circumstances that I had no control over.

House Of Cards

As time went by, no matter how hard I tried to resolve my emotional issues, I'd get triggered when I least expected it, and they'd come back stronger. And, whether I'd like to admit it or not, motherhood had taken its toll on me, even more so because of the loss.

I thought my life would be better with time and financial prosperity, especially because I had someone by my side who loved me and did his utmost to look after me. I also had the affection of my husband's family who treated me like a daughter and were very welcoming.

However, parental abandonment still haunted my unconscious and the traumas were instilled within me, such as the difficulty in controlling my emotions and dealing with adversity, leading me to the idea of failure and frustration. I didn't know how to deal with the circumstances.

No matter how hard I tried, I couldn't show affection in return. I also struggled internally with wanting to be loved, but my way of expressing affection was pushing people away.

I only came to understand what I was feeling after a long time and with self-knowledge. It's very important to recognize the aspects of our personality that we use most, identify neglected or unknown traits, and heal them.

As a physical and energetic body, we need to deal with the imbalance of our extremes. Our emotional energy is highly connected and built on the foundation of our physical energy state.

So, if we're in a state of passivity or too much control, we need to rebalance our emotional energy. Taking care of the physical body, having contact with nature, observing physical bodily signs, and working on specific emotions helps with energy harmonization.

The *yin-yang* theory[1] used in Traditional Chinese Medicine describes the dynamic between the body and the environment to treat physical and psychological illnesses. It explains a lot about the movement of the two forces that favor change, then unified in harmony. The Yin symbolizes the dark, water, intuition, and the ability to nourish life. The Yang constitutes the luminous, fire, impetuous, and expansion.

This philosophy would eventually inspire the psychoanalyst Carl Jung (1875-1961) when developing his method. According to him: men tend to think and judge only as men. Women tend to think and act only as women. However, psychological facts show

---

1 The exact origin of the yin-yang theory is unknown, but the first reference appears in the Book of Changes, around 700 BC. The concept became popular in the 3rd century BC with the work of the Chinese school of Yinyang, led by the cosmologist Zou Yan. This theory, which influenced religion, philosophy, medicine, and calligraphy, is one of the pillars of Taoism and represents duality, i.e. the idea that positive and negative are complementary and not opposites. The yin-yang theory is based on the idea that everything in the universe is the result of the interaction between these two opposite states.

that we all have well-defined aspects of our personality.

For Jung, the functioning of the psyche originates from the tension between opposites. On one hand, one polarity is considered feminine, and on the other, it is considered masculine. This duality is the necessary condition for growth and maturation.

The polarity considered feminine that interacts with emotions nurtures, welcomes, gives, and cares. When we listen to our intuition, we are in touch with this polarity. In this way, we accept the end of certain cycles and the start of new ones as part of our learning process. The polarity considered masculine is present in our logical and rational aspects. We become independent, competitive, and decision-makers.

Throughout human history, many beliefs have been spread about women for fear of the strength they bring through their ability to generate another being in their womb. This can be proven by various studies, even seen in the first drawings of Paleolithic man.

These beliefs implanted in women establish a set of values and standards to which they were subjected, such as expectations of fragility and weakness. However, with the various revolutions and wars, many women had to abandon this role to take on jobs in the labor market alongside men, or even as the breadwinner of the household when their husbands were incapacitated by battles.

This put an emotional and physical strain on women, who started working inside and outside the home, worrying about finances, raising children, and supporting their partners. Not to mention the cases of single mothers and widows. Many of them struggled to express honest and intimate feelings due to a lack of time and space to express themselves.

Considering the neuroscience, psychology, and psychoanalysis studies, there is work aimed at feminine reconnection since many qualities related to feminine energy have been exalted in recent years, such as empathy, affection, welcomeness, and vulnerability. These qualities must be exercised so that people and the society they are a part of can heal their pain and create a better world for the next generations.

As soon as I began to understand this relationship, I realized that in the presence and the community of other women, we identify ourselves with each other and grow, without having to compete.

However, until I became aware of this healing process, I positioned myself as a victim of my circumstances. I blamed the other person for my emotional state without realizing that I would need to accept myself first to be able to help those who were by my side.

I wanted to be recognized for my potential, but I didn't take on the protagonist role in my story. Every time I looked in the mirror, I saw my image reflected, but I didn't recognize myself. I had faith, courage, and trust, but I didn't value my self-esteem or accept what was imposed on me as a possibility for new paths.

I was afraid of judgment, social pressure, and losing my husband. I constantly compared myself to others which made me feel inferior. This reinforced a concept I didn't understand until later: if I deny it, I come closer to it. Through this, I lost myself in my values and principles.

However, I didn't give up hope. In the depths of my heart, I knew I had something bigger prepared in my life. I needed to learn and set off in search of authority and autonomy while learning how to deal with my shadows, especially abandonment.

CHAPTER 4

THE SECOND LEAP: FROM SÃO PAULO TO THE WORLD

Towards A New Dream

"What excellent hands you have, girl!"

This was the phrase I often heard when I massaged someone or treated their skin in a cosmetic procedure. For six months, I surprised myself by working with my friend at the beauty clinic.

In one of my conversations with clients, I learned that a salon in the Butantã neighborhood had rooms available. I rented one and invested in basic equipment, such as a stretcher, chair, support tables, and products. As I couldn't afford to study cosmetology at a university, I continued to take free technical courses in esthetics. These courses helped me greatly in my work with the treatments.

I stayed at the Butantã space for two years. Then another opportunity came up. Thanks to a client who liked my work I was invited to a salon in *Itaim Bibi*, a noble neighborhood in São Paulo, to work with esthetics for an elite São Paulo clientele of successful and influential people from television, radio, and magazines. At the time, social media wasn't yet so widespread.

Coming into contact with people with a privileged academic background not only helped me grow professionally regarding the quality of my procedures but also made me smarter financially and as an entrepreneur. It was a completely new world unfolding in front of me every day. Because people liked my work, my name began to be known in the esthetics industry, no longer as Cleudiana but as **Cleo Pillon**.

Those were years of great learning. I discovered that, in addition to massages and esthetics, people enjoyed talking to me. Somehow, I was doing good for those I was serving, which was very gratifying. That was the start of a life project I still couldn't materialize, but I was already preparing for the big leap.

My life progressed daily, and this progress manifested in material terms. My husband and I decided to buy a house in Granja Viana, a neighborhood on the west side of Greater São Paulo. It was one of the happiest moments of my life. At that moment, I realized owning a home had been another dream. Now, I could say that I made it come true.

But the emotional wounds from childhood that hadn't been dealt with until then started to take shape when I became pregnant again. As I'd had a miscarriage with my previous pregnancy, I was already showing signs of peripartum syndrome, so my obstetrician recommended I rest until the end of the pregnancy.

With my husband's support and following the doctor's instructions, I stopped working in the esthetics industry and stayed home to rest. However, I'd never stood still in my life.

To pass the time, I would watch TV shows about human behavior, a topic that had always interested me. The issue was that I was following the analysis of cases of serial killers and psychopaths, which made the shadows in my own life begin to gain a voice once again. As a result, I began to develop a panic disorder.

I felt afraid to go outside my house, or when I needed to go to a doctor's appointment. I was often frightened by people's behavior, and this fed a dark side that I tried not to see for years. When I needed to be hospitalized for some reason, I felt safer. But when I returned home, the fear began to take hold of me.

When you lack the self-knowledge to accept and redefine your pain, the road to success will be full of victories and defeats. However, I wasn't yet mature enough to understand this important aspect and fell victim to my unhealed wounds.

Little by little, I began to isolate myself without realizing it. I demanded too much of my husband by creating situations that didn't exist beyond my own perception. I noticed he began to distance himself from me, which caused even more insecurity. No matter how hard I tried, I couldn't cope with what was happening to me.

After giving birth, realizing that I was losing control of the situation, I began to take a stand and face my fears, even though I was still quite fragile emotionally and without psychological help. I hired a nanny to support me with the baby's initial care and returned to work.

I believed that if I were working, all the emotional symptoms would dissipate over time. After all, the cosmetic procedures were like therapy, and talking to people made me feel better.

I started to get better and no longer felt so many symptoms when I was away from home. Because I dreamt of having a professional space, my husband helped me invest in a beauty clinic with a salon.

To further reinforce my transformation, I joined a gym to eliminate the extra 60 pounds I had gained during pregnancy. It was there that I met a personal trainer, who would become not just a guide, but a great friend.

As my physical body strengthened, my emotional body also responded faster. Work and gym training were great for me. At that moment, I began to understand that self-development is impossible without self-knowledge, which is the basis of my life project.

If I had been aware of this process then, I wouldn't have lost so much. In the essence of my being, welcoming my shadows and managing my emotions is the power of transformation because they activate my potential for life. Change needed to come from me. Not from someone else. However, learning this is a process, and not every process is easy to experience.

Broken Alliances

After 13 years of a relationship, my marriage came to an end. As everything happened in such a troubled way, I didn't realize that I was losing myself and my husband. I can't deny that he tried to help me, but I closed myself off and only saw what my wounded inner self wanted to see.

As my personal trainer and friend planned to enter the television world, she began preparing for a new path. However, with her departure towards stardom came the promise that she wanted me to be her executive assistant as soon as she boosted her career.

While she sought fame, I decided to study cosmetology at a private college in São Paulo. A new stage in my life began, in which I learned from the course and the techniques. I can say that I was one of the best students in my class. I was constantly called to the front of the class to explain a procedure because I had so much experience.

As I excelled in my university courses, I realized that my knowledge brought recognition and even a certain authority. However, internal unresolved emotional feelings caused me to feel like I was losing myself.

After our divorce, my ex-husband and I decided to sell our house. With part of the proceeds, I bought another home in the same proportion and financed the remaining amount equivalent to the purchase.

With the earnings from the beauty clinic, I could cover the mortgage, car, and household costs, while also covering the expenses of the housekeeper and nanny. But lack of financial planning was still an issue linked to my emotional healing, even though I wasn't in a position to realize this at the time.

It was then that my friend's promise came true. She wanted me by her side as an executive assistant. Since I was divorced and had the support of the nanny and my sister to look after my son, I decided I couldn't miss out on this opportunity. Although the financial income would be less than at the clinic, I craved recognition and accepted the offer. After all, the moment I had been waiting for had arrived.

A Shooting Star

From that day on, my life changed completely. It was trip after trip, the hottest parties, and the most unbelievable events imaginable. My friend shone and I followed her everywhere, all while caring for her beauty and looks. I barely had time to go home and be with my son. Her schedule was always packed, and I had to keep up with her.

However, I was 32 and no longer had the same energy as before. To stay awake all night, I started taking stimulants. It was the only way I would stay up. In financial terms, the reduction in my earnings began to limit my spending, and I ended up delaying some bills. But I couldn't turn back now. After all, having this life was what I'd always dreamed of, and my esthetics clinic had someone else in charge.

Initially, it was the thrill of being in the company of extremely wealthy and well-known individuals in the media, attending the best parties, dinners, balls, and events. Over time, however, the routine began to take its toll. Ingesting stimulants combined with a drink or two had many side effects on my body. The yo-yo effect was one of them, which I solved with more medication for rapid weight loss.

When I had the chance to go home, I felt an overwhelming sense of emptiness. In those moments, I realized how much I was repeating everything I had experienced and suffered in childhood because of my mother's absence. Without realizing it, I was repeating the same pattern with my son. When he saw me, he would throw himself into my arms as if begging for a bit of affection and a mother's love.

My heart was torn when I had to leave him. But I couldn't stop at that moment. There was a commitment to my work that required my constant attention. However, everything that hadn't been resolved resurfaced. Many feelings of inferiority surrounded my thoughts and I struggled to retaliate.

The problem was that with low income came material losses. The first to go was my car. At the time, a friend offered me money to pay the installments on the car, but I refused. It was my problem, and I had to solve it. My heart was in pieces the day the dealership picked up the car at my house.

Then, my house went up for auction because I had delayed paying the installments. The debts were piling up, and I couldn't pay them off. But it was different when it came to my house because I had my son. How could I leave my son without a home to live in? I accepted the help of a friend to cover the late payments and avoid having my house auctioned off.

My emotional state was getting worse and worse. The sleepless nights, the excess of stimulants, and drinks at parties started to become part of my life. As well as the antidepressants. I was losing more and more of who I was and what I believed in.

For six years, I lived this unruly life, I was lost in a world that wasn't mine as I was enveloped in a reality that didn't belong to me and that I thought brought happiness. A grand illusion that took me back to the encounter of my shadows.

Now and then, I'd hear a voice whisper in my heart that I needed to rescue myself and have faith in who I was. In those moments, I remembered my father and Altair, our times at church, and how hard they tried to protect me from this world I was giving myself over to more and more.

I gradually reduced my time as my friend's assistant and took on temporary side jobs to earn more income, mainly with people I knew and reality TV show stars who were gaining recognition at the time.

But even so, the routine of events was constant and took up much of my life. I was already almost forty years old, and my son was growing up without his mother's presence. Then, in a chance encounter, a proposal renewed my hope.

The Microphone Is Yours

I was attending an event when a well-known broadcaster approached me. He said he'd been looking for me for some time because he was launching a new project and wanted me to be part of it. I responded that I knew nothing about radio and TV except as a celebrity executive assistant.

He explained that he had initially considered my friend but changed his mind when he met me and talked briefly to me at another event. He also said the project was still a pilot and would work alongside two incredible hosts if I did well in the audition.

Another opportunity opened up in my life, and I embraced it with all my energy. I did the audition and passed. *Festa da Band* (Band's Party) was a live program on *Rádio Bandeirantes* that aired at noon on Saturdays and Sundays. Alongside performances of country music, funk, and other styles, they would conduct interviews with popular singers of the time. My microphone was real this time, and the interviews were very popular.

At first, there were three hosts: me and two well-known broadcasters. Then, it shifted to just me and one of the broadcasters. The program was entertaining and had a large audience when it aired, mainly because of audience participation. Financially, I didn't have a salary. We made money through sponsorships. Because of the high viewership, we had quite a few sponsors.

I hosted this program for three years and learned much about radio communication. I confess: it was a wonderful experience in my life because I became even better known among celebrities and the general public.

As the program was on weekends at lunchtime, I dedicated the rest of my week to consulting work. I had contracts to fulfill and couldn't leave people without my support.

The work was exhausting, but with the extra income, I could settle my debts, including those with my friend who helped me with the installments on my house. I've always been committed to honoring those who helped me. Additionally, I could save money to make other plans and guarantee my son's future.

As time passed, the anguish bothered me even more because I deviated from my path. I felt tired, alone, and guilty for not being with my son. So, I reconnected with my inner self and the strength that inhabits our being. In prayer, I asked to find a way out of that loneliness and get back on my path. I also wanted to find someone to look after me and my son, who could love me and my little one to form a family.

I then realized I craved a home, a family, a partner, and love. I was giving too much of myself to people and not enough to myself, which was hurting me. I needed to find myself again amidst the shadows and put the pieces back together to rewrite my story.

Energetic (Re)Connections

Because I knew many people from different industries, friends would often come to me to help them with some intermediation to sell products or make partnerships. I was always helpful, brought people together, and promoted interesting opportunities. That's how I met my current husband: by brokering deals.

The businessman who participated in the negotiation was American and was going through a challenging divorce. So we started talking about our lives and everything we were going through and became friends.

The closeness of the meeting and the negotiations brought us closer together, and a mutual feeling emerged. We needed each other, and we were ready for a fresh start.

From the first time I saw him, something inside me told me he was the man I wanted by my side. We shared the same goals of living our dreams. Like me, he had experienced a troubled life, so we spoke the same language and shared the same needs.

A simply charming man, concerned about me, affectionate, and a companion. By his side, I found support, security, and a lot of love. He enveloped me in a very special way, and I feel fulfilled and complete by his side. I'm sure that God prepared our meeting so that we could follow a new path of life and mutual healing.

The only thing that separated us was distance. I still had work commitments in Brazil, and he had his business in the United States. However, we both had an immense desire to be together and experience the love growing between us daily.

Superhero Signs

With each circumstance that came up, I realized how emotionally unbalanced I was. No matter how hard I tried to deal with conflicts, they took shape and became even bigger enemies. Until this moment, I hadn't yet considered psychological treatment or any therapeutic work, and this was further compromising my life in every way.

The consequences of parental abandonment manifested themselves in my behavior: exaggerated distrust, excessive jealousy, and possessive behavior. These behaviors were what happened in my relationship with my ex-husband. It was a chaotic lifestyle like the one I lived during my celebrity consultant days, filled with depression, anxiety, low self-esteem, self-deprecation, and lack of self-love, all while searching for someone or something (professional fulfillment) to fill the existential void.

In an attempt to deal with my conflicts, I unconsciously adopted the superhero syndrome, and the signs I mentioned were proof of that. I positioned myself as a savior: someone who worried about everything and everyone except myself.

In reality, this superhero was searching for belonging, acceptance, and a way to be noticed by others. She wanted to make up for the lack of affection her mother's abandonment caused her. The lonely girl who locked her emotions away in imaginary boxes grew up without affection, without recognizing herself in front of the mirror or before herself. She was emotionally sick and her body was debilitated by trying to camouflage the bleeding wounds.

The moment I stripped myself of this heroine and all my warrior armor, I got down on my knees before the Creator and asked him for an antidote to remove the poison that was eating away at my insides and causing me so much emotional pain. With an open heart, I begged him to take me into his arms, to give me support, a motherly lap, and to help me reconnect with my purpose in life so that I could be strengthened and support my son.

I was completely introspective about myself and my inner voice at that moment. I realized that I needed to recover the protagonism in my story, take a few steps back, and reclaim myself so that I could resume my journey, strengthened by my essence.

But for that to happen, I had to complete the most important task: learn to forgive. Forgiving the person who abandoned me would allow me to heal my traumas. Only then did I realize that I needed help from a professional who could guide me on the path to inner healing.

Through therapy, I've come to understand that forgiving doesn't mean accepting a bad event but rather allowing the negative emotions associated with it to disappear once and for all. It's the only way to find or build a path forward to being open to happiness and new experiences.

It's not easy. Only with techniques and extensive knowledge from professionals can you free yourself from the past, deal with your uncertainties, and experience emotional discomfort to recognize what makes you happy and live a more conscious life.

But while I was going through the process, the duality was still present, and I had to deal with all the emotions that came up in the circumstances that enveloped me with the same intensity. If on the one hand, I was filled with happiness in my relationship, then on the other hand, my concern for my father also took on the same proportion.

CHAPTER 5

THE THIRD LEAP: LEARNING TO EMBRACE MY EMOTIONS

My Dad, My Hero

Despite all the difficulties and excessive work, I never distanced myself from my family and did my utmost to support them. I've always believed that I would only progress if I respected the people who came before me.

After I left *Imperatriz* for São Paulo, my father and Altair moved to *Carolina do Maranhão*. As well as being smaller and quieter, Altair would be close to her family. My father dreamed of living somewhere quieter to enjoy his old age better.

Around the age of fifty, he became diabetic and had to stop traveling by truck, mainly because of his eyesight. According to the doctors, being overworked, lacking a healthy diet, and having sleepless nights due to the long routine on the roads as a driver led to physical exhaustion.

Because he worked for a large company and the goods he was transporting had to be at a specific place on the appointed day, he had to stay awake to cover long stretches of road and ensure he didn't get into an accident on the way. Therefore, he used stimulants to stay awake and focused on driving.

At first, he attributed the severe pain he felt in his back to the time he spent sitting behind the wheel of the truck and the repetitive movements of his legs and feet. Over time and after a series of tests, he discovered that he had a kidney problem.

Even with intense treatment, his kidneys didn't work again, so the doctors recommended hemodialysis. When I heard about his physical condition, I did my utmost to help, even taking him to see some specialists in São Paulo.

Unfortunately, the town he lived in didn't have many health resources. To undergo hemodialysis three times a week, my father traveled in a van with 14 other people from *Carolina do Maranhão* to *Imperatriz*, which had more hospitals and medical treatment options. The journey took three hours one way and three hours back.

I sent him money for food and his living expenses. I also gave financial aid to my mother and helped my brothers as best I could. I knew in the back of my mind that my father's state of health would potentially worsen over time. I didn't lose faith but knew that would happen according to God's will.

I often talked to him and my brothers by video call because I had to travel a lot for work. His health had deteriorated since I had last seen him. In addition to the poor results of the hemodialysis, he suffered a heart attack and was in the ICU of a hospital in *Imperatriz*.

I couldn't waste any more time. I needed to be with him before he left for spirituality. He was my father, and I loved him very much. I knew how happy he would be with my presence, so I rescheduled my appointments and set off for the airport. Because I was outside Brazil, the flight would take longer.

In my prayers, I asked my father to hold on a little longer. While connecting from one airport to another, I organized my brothers and nephews to be present with him. I also got my son to go with me to visit his grandfather.

During the journey, I talked to my father in my head, and I realized how much I loved him and the importance of everything he taught me. He was always by my side, even when life's challenges wore me down. His words encouraged me to stand firm and not abandon my dreams.

His words have stayed in my memory, and whenever I think back on them, they envelop me in love and confidence. I just have to believe that nothing can stop me.

"Go on, my child! Don't give up! I believe in you!"

During the trip to *Imperatriz*, I remembered when I was a child and how much I admired my father when he arrived with the huge truck. The superhero imagery was never lost from my memory, even when I argued with him at the gate of my mother's house.

Deep down, I also felt abandoned by my father because he spent so much time working away from home. The same feeling I had when my mother left was also reflected in my father. I only came to understand this a long time later with therapy.

I knew that my proactivity, the will that drove me to go beyond my limits, to face the darkness and dangers of life, came from him. Like my father, I dream of conquering the world. I feel an immense need to explore new places and find myself.

The image I saw on that ICU bed was of an aged man, weak and swollen because of his kidney problem, but who contained, in his essence, my childhood hero.

When he saw me, he opened his eyes and said proudly:

"That's my little girl, my youngest!"

My father had an affectionate way of calling me that I loved. He used to say: "Oh, my little girl!"

I stayed with him for four days during hospital visiting hours. He was happy I took my siblings and my son to see him. I will always remember my son's meeting with my father. It was a demonstration of respect and affection between generations.

The name Pedro echoes through time, strong and timeless, in homage to my father. Like his grandfather, my son carries great meaning and admirable attributes.

On the fourth day, when I said goodbye to him to return to my routine with a heavy heart, I approached his ear and said, almost whispering:

"You were the best father in the world!"

On an impulse, I corrected my speech:

"You are the best father in the world!"

At that moment, I thought about hugging him once more, but I pulled back. I was too emotional. I should have hugged him. He left sometime after our meeting. I still spoke to him a few times by video call, but I hardly heard his voice. He was getting weaker every day. He was discharged from the hospital and spent some time in the house I had rented in the city.

On his last birthday, we talked for a while. It was Christmas Eve, but there was a lot of anguish in my chest. It's hard to see someone you love suffering.

Even though he couldn't speak much, he told me slowly:

"My little girl, I love you very much and will always be by your side!"

When I received the news of my father's death, although I was emotional, I understood that it was time for him to go and that, in a way, only his body was dying. In spirit, he would always be with me. He is half of who I am.

At that moment, I understood that my father did the best he could for his children and loved each one in his own way. I thanked him for the opportunity he had given me to be his daughter and for everything he had taught me. "Dad, I forgive you! I love you so much! I'm grateful for everything you've given me, including my life! You will always be in my heart!".

Me, The Protagonist

"What's your name?"
"Cleo Pillon."
"Where are you from?
"Brazil."
"What do you want to do here?"
"Change my life, embrace my identity, and recognize my potential and competence."

I was having this conversation with myself as I enjoyed the slow movement of the waters of the Long Island River, which cuts through New York City. One of the tourist attractions I consider most beautiful is the city of Long Island.

The feeling I had at that moment was one of gratitude. I was finally learning to look at life differently, stripped of armor or any clothing to camouflage my appearance. It was only me and my truth at that moment.

How fascinating that encounter was! I was part of myself, the master of my life, and not hiding from anyone or anything. Little by little, my little boxes of feelings began to open so that I could take in all the emotions I had let go unnoticed.

Gratitude also came in the form of forgiveness for myself, my past, my father, and my mother. My father's departure took much of our history with him, but it showed how much love can do for people. The most beautiful lesson he left us was forgiveness for my mother, who was by his side until his death.

Over time, he and Altair split up. So my brother Rui went to live with him to support him when he was ill, as did my mother and Altair from time to time.

When I took on the protagonist role, my finances also began

to adjust. An inner switch went off and woke me up to reality. I soon understood that there is no prosperity in the feeling of lack. The partnership I established between friends began to generate income because I learned to value what I promoted and myself.

After all, leadership means taking responsibility and taking charge of your life and career, taking control and acknowledging the consequences of conscious choices, while understanding your unconscious choices. To understand this is to co-create surprising situations in your life.

Little by little, I realized that accepting my emotions, without judging them or fearing the feelings they would bring me, was the first step towards my healing. Fear, anger, anguish, and other emotions that I considered to be weaknesses in my actions or that even led to frustration had a role to play in my emotional learning.

By hiding them in my imaginary boxes, I injected a poison that made them take on frightening shapes. The shadows that, time and again, came back to haunt me. These shadows became sabotaging behaviors in my professional life, relationships, and myself, as if they were eating away the best of me.

When I learned to welcome my emotions with empathy, I began to honor my true self and became a better person. I found ease within myself, dialoging with each sensation I felt to alleviate my pain and show it that I was being welcomed with love.

The first step I took toward change was to allow the emotion I was feeling to surface so that it would no longer catch me off guard or take on a proportion I didn't want. To strengthen myself, I would try to isolate myself for a few minutes, and without fearing what people would think of me, I would calm down and initiate an internal dialogue.

The second step was to name the emotion (sadness, anguish,

anger, possessiveness, etc.) present and ask the following questions: "Where are you from? Are you associated with something? Which part of me is affected? Where do you affect me physically, and in what way?" As I asked the questions, I kept an eye on which part of my body showed a reaction or what came to mind.

In the third step, I linked the emotion I was feeling to other emotions, thoughts, and events from my personal history. Again, I asked the following questions: "What other time have I felt this way? What was the context? What do the contexts have in common?" I discovered the unconscious pattern that was repeating itself.

In the fourth step, I redefined the emotion to establish an association with my entire life story. At this point, I saw myself as a protagonist, no longer as a victim, canceling out the effects some of the negative emotions had on my life.

Yes, I Accept

Feeling stronger every day, the sequence of events came as a gift from the Universe as a marriage proposal in front of the Long Island City postcard. My fiancé, on one knee with a passionate look on his face, wanted me by his side.

Without hesitation, I answered:

"Yes, my love, I accept! Today and for the rest of my life! I accept being by your side, living this love that gives me many wonderful sensations."

With the waters of the Hudson River as our accomplice, that moment sealed a new phase in my life. This time, I was ready to truly live my love story with a "happily ever after" every day because there was complicity in our passionate souls.

After a few months, we began preparing to celebrate our union with family and some dear friends before God and for all eternity. I couldn't contain my happiness at everything I was experiencing and yet to experience. I was sure that this was the life I wanted and the place I wanted to be.

I chose a wonderful white wedding dress for the ceremony that took place at City Hall in Manhattan. I took care of every detail so that the moment would be perfect, just like my plans for my life from that day on.

Our story featured not only love but also our children. At first, we had to reconcile all the challenges that could have caused conflicts, but I was preparing to deal emotionally with the new situation.

Moving to another country requires adapting to a new culture and language. Additionally, each of us brings our own unique stories, customs, and values. Reconciling all these elements takes time, patience, and a lot of dialogue to adjust to the rhythm of this new life.

I couldn't travel or leave the country because I had to wait for a residence visa. I also couldn't bring my son to live with me because he was completing his basic education in Brazil. So, for a few months, we had to be physically separated.

Little by little, I learned to live with my six stepchildren (three from the first marriage and three from the second). As there were differences in culture, habits, and expectations, I was constantly being tested, but it was in this process that I discovered my true strength.

Unlike the other times, something inside told me I had to react and change the situation. For many years, I had been through good and bad experiences, a divorce, a life that wasn't truly mine, accompanying so many people, and contributing in one way or another to many stories. Now was my chance to live my life with more knowledge.

So, with resilience, love, and acceptance, everything found its place. Over time, it was gratifying to see the closeness between father and children, in a relationship of love, empathy, and welcoming.

A year after our wedding, the eldest daughter from his second marriage came to live with us, and eventually, his son joined us. I felt like an eagle developing the ability to love, care, and welcome these children in ways I had never imagined. Today, we are one big, happy family, celebrating life and love every day.

Being loved and cherished by my husband's children is one of my greatest blessings. My son, Pedro, has gained sibling friends. When I see everyone sitting around the table in our family gatherings, I feel a sense of gratitude for everything we've built together.

> "A wife of noble character who can find? She is worth far more than rubies. Her husband has full confidence in her and lacks nothing of value. She brings him good, not harm, all the days of her life." Proverbs 31: 10-12 says.

Today, I have learned to face my shadows, especially those of pride, authoritarianism, arrogance, and selfishness. I've also learned not to take on roles that don't belong to me. Respect for myself and others must be an agreement renewed every day, and only in this way will we avoid frustration and disappointment.

I realized I'm not always right, mainly because we have unique paths, choices, and opinions. I also realized that I can remain silent in times of tribulation. That peace I was looking for is now what I have. In God, I have learned the value of my essence.

My marriage was one of my greatest leaps in healing the wounds that I still carried. I am immensely grateful for the caring, loving, and respectful husband that God has given me. He is my friend, companion, and partner for all hours.

Camera, Action "In English, Please"

More financially established, harmonious in my marriage, and adapted to my new life, I began researching how to build a new business in the industry I had trained in: esthetics.

As I was not yet fluent in English, I asked a friend to help me translate short texts and practice my pronunciation to produce short videos for social media. I aimed to create a sequence explaining the importance of aesthetic facial treatments.

My idea was to use my knowledge to teach others how to clean their skin at home, promoting the importance of applying creams, the right way to massage the face, and how to get the best results. I would always focus on well-being, not just vanity.

With this action, I resumed my proactivity, a skill I had developed since childhood. I soon gained followers who liked my skincare proposals and how I worked with the products. Before long, cosmetic brands sought me out to promote their portfolio. I was once again involved in what I loved so much.

CHAPTER 6

THE FOURTH LEAP: UNDERSTANDING THE VALUE OF HELP

Gua-Sha: The First Tool Of A New Era

I aimed to expand my work with aesthetic products, as more and more companies were seeking me out for advertising partnerships on social media. My idea was to create a product with my characteristics. I saw this as a great business opportunity.

But then the COVID-19 pandemic came, followed by social isolation—a difficult time with many uncertainties. We didn't know what would happen the next day. We had to re-plan our entire lives and daily life became another challenge. We couldn't leave the house for a while to socialize in the open air or chat with others. We needed a new strategy to deal with our accumulated emotions.

Noticing people's needs in the face of isolation, such as virtual companionship and good messages to help them cope at a time when death and human suffering were constantly being seen on the news and social media, I increased the messages of energy, strength, external beauty and faith in my videos. I wanted to be a channel for people to feel less alone. I realized how much good it was doing by the incredible response I received.

Then, I returned to the idea of creating a product. But I found it difficult because I couldn't travel or have face-to-face meetings. So I started studying to see how I could make something that would do people good without needing a lot of investment and research. This is when the *Gua-Sha* emerged—a natural therapeutic tool with many benefits.

The base of the Gua-Sha is a stone from ancient Chinese medicine, the Bian, which has various shapes and residues of different materials. This stone has self-healing power and is easy to sanitize due to its anatomical shape.

I already had the product designed, but I now needed a brand name and a company to work with me on mass-producing it for sale. I wanted a name that referred to my strength, faith, and desire to win that had been with me since childhood. I also wanted the brand to represent the idea of empowerment.

For many days, I drew up various names for the brand, but none met what I wanted. One day while browsing the internet, I came across a reference to a shield of Zeus known as the Aegis. In Greek mythology, Zeus was presented with this shield by his daughter Athena, which represented strength, resistance, and protection.

With the shield, Zeus fought the Titans and all his enemies in great battles. The Aegis was considered a very strong weapon because it was indestructible. And there it was. I found the name of my brand: Aegisderma, referencing "Aegis" in reference to the shield and "derma" for skin.

An American company founded by a Brazilian with the mission of offering more love and care for the skin. It was a dream come true, showing that my attitude of transformation was providing notoriety and recognition. After all, Aegisderma is for those who believe in self-love. When we understand who we are, we choose the best for ourselves.

Even in isolation at home, I contacted a few companies to pitch my product to and began registering the Aegisderma trademark. As I stepped out of the victim role, the circumstances lined up in my favor. Soon after, I was sharing my product on social media.

Gua-Sha was a hit because it promotes a caressing sensation on the skin while stimulating circulation, producing collagen, reducing swelling and inflammation, firming the skin, brightening the complexion, releasing tension, and shaping the facial muscles. To date, it is one of the best-selling products on the site.

Creating my brand and my first product was a dream come true. I felt fulfilled in every way. I was happy in my marriage, and my son and I were getting closer. Therapy helped me face the beliefs and fears that visited me from time to time.

When we dare to work on what prevents us from understanding who we are and the shadows of the past, especially childhood, we become better people and avoid many mistakes we made in old relationships. Thus, more empowered, I began reframing my feelings when I felt insecure about my husband and son. I was breaking the cycle of beliefs that I had brought from my childhood and my ancestry.

This was very positive because I realized that, in most cases, my inner child wanted to replace adult Cleo and would lose herself altogether. By embracing my true essence, I also understood that I established conditions for fulfillment and prosperity to be present without the need to use money to compensate for emotional issues.

I knew that inside my heart, when I was awake and ready to receive healing, I would be blessed and given a new chance. I opened myself to true love and divine blessings in this encounter between soul and essence.

Reprogramming the beliefs that limited me wasn't easy at all, and it's an exercise I have practiced until today because I understand that our evolution requires consistency and discipline in everything we set out to do. Everything from implementing new habits to adhering to healthy behaviors requires a lot of willpower, perseverance, courage, and commitment.

Armed with this strength, I no longer feared my shadows. Without fear, I let them come to the surface so I could understand where the feeling was coming from and work on giving it a positive meaning, like a boost of life.

Awakening to this reality is transformative. It means using your potential to build better relationships and taking charge of your life, no longer victimizing yourself. It means taking your place as the protagonist and no longer the supporting actor in your life story. Only in this way do we learn to forgive truly. We tend to see ourselves and the other person in their essence, outside of the judgments that distance us from each other. This process requires daily discipline so we can maintain our path fairly.

That's how I understood why my mother left when we were still children. She didn't abandon us, as I had always thought in my emotional memory. She left behind her unhappiness and the emotional pain she felt, and had no resources to alleviate.

In this way, I also understood my father's reasons when he educated us more harshly. I accepted my reality and took control of my life with authority, no longer as a succession of invalidated experiences.

By being aware of this process, I could help others make the journey less painful and achieve more. Based on this, I put into practice the following concept: *I grow and can contribute to the growth of others because my dream of growth and fulfillment drives me.*

And that barefoot girl from *Imperatriz*, in *Maranhão*, became an entrepreneur known for the quality of her products and investments in other industries. Now she could say that she was part of the constellation of stars that inspired her to dream that one day she would cross the world in high heels, not just as someone in the background parading her looks, but as a woman in the process of healing from her emotional pain, ready to follow her purpose of transforming more women into stars too.

As the acceptance of my first product grew, so did sales, and some partnership proposals from American companies to create other products in the area began to appear. I began new studies to see what the next launch could be like and came up with a blend. After some information that I should choose an American company to be better accepted by the clientele, I opted for one of them to expose the product to the market.

Unfortunately, the second launch failed, not because of the quality of the product but because of my lack of experience as an entrepreneur. The company that promoted my brand scammed me by offering only a small percentage, changing the product's name, and marketing it as if it were theirs. Three months later, when I discovered the commercial plot, I deleted the product from the site since no one had signed any contracts.

I must confess that when I learned about the company scam, I was devastated, but didn't victimize myself. What happened instigated me to seek better training and understanding of this business environment to be more effective.

With emotional support, I decided to change my strategy. Instead of looking for another American company, I invested in a Brazilian company to develop a new product and launched it on the American market shortly afterward. The goal was for the Aegisderma brand to expand its portfolio and begin to be noticed in the cosmetics industry.

Sales increased, and so did confidence in the Brazilian company. It was time to give life to a childhood dream: a cosmetics line aimed at self-love. That's how the ERA line was born, whose name represented the new phase I was living in.

After all, a new era brings transformation and increases

self-esteem, which is reflected in all aspects of life, including the skin. With the slogan "a new ERA for your skin", Aegisderma gained more self-care and self-esteem products.

I also promoted with each launch, using my image and profile as a businesswoman. Thanks to my entrepreneurship and my process of self-development, success was present. I was demonstrating my dominance as a specialist in esthetics.

With exposure at specialized trade fairs, I was ready for Aegisderma's first and biggest market launch. The doors opened to expose my product to companies outside the US, and I was very committed to it.

"Salto Alto Connection": The Project

It was time to implement a project I'd been planning for a few years but had been putting off. I started sketching out a pilot plan for a women's program. The idea was to use my background and experiences in different contexts to encourage people to be the best versions of themselves.

To make the program truly transformative, I participated in several immersion courses focused on emotional intelligence. I hired mentors who could help me delve deeper into human behavior. I connected with health professionals, such as psychologists, therapists, and other specialists, so that we could bring psychological guidance and quality of life to the people taking part in the training. The program was designed to be transformative for those who participated in it.

This is how *"Salto Alto Connection"* (The Big Leap)

emerged. The first two versions of the project were online and free. Once the model was ready, it was monetized to expand the quality of the offerings. The project's idea was to promote activities that could highlight women's weaknesses and redefine them through an exchange of experiences.

To expand the project further, I created the *Salto Alto Podcast*, a space open to Brazilian immigrants to share stories of overcoming obstacles in America. As I have a lot to teach and learn, the project is an incredible opportunity to get to know each other.

However, as much as I had worked on my emotions, I remember that a lack of recognition momentarily paralyzed me two weeks before the Move for Women *Salto Alto Connection* in-person event.

At that moment, I thought about giving up on the event. Thoughts like: "I can't. I can't bring this knowledge to women. I'm not strong enough" wandered through my mind and made me procrastinate and hide from everything. That feeling couldn't get any stronger inside me. So, I decided to look in the mirror to dispel the feeling of not recognizing my worth.

And it was before my reflected image that my father's encouraging words came to mind:

"Daughter, you can do anything you want. You're strong. Don't be afraid, I'm by your side."

At that moment, I felt empowered, as if my father were encouraging me not to give up. I had come so far in my goals and couldn't abandon everything now.

"Yes, Dad. I'm strong. I'm brave, and I'm not going to give up now, for both of us," I responded to myself.

The event was much better than I expected. At the end of the event, I paid a beautiful tribute to my father and shared about the moment I had experienced a week earlier. I'm sure he was by my side in spirit, holding my hand and not letting me give up.

From all this, I've learned that we're in this world to make our dreams come true and to contribute to others. We have the right to be happy and to develop ourselves as people. The "Salto Alto Connection" event taught me this. I'm very grateful for the journey I experienced with over a hundred other women.

Today, I learn daily to manage and face my shadows, not to take on roles that don't belong to me, and to value my essence, supported by divine wisdom. Thus, I allow myself to be happy and make others happy.

When I was 17, my suitcase contained faith and courage, along with a few clothes. Now, it is full of fulfilled dreams, prosperity, and a lot of love for the story I've written along the way.

CHAPTER 7

"SALTO ALTO CONNECTION": THE TRIAD OF ESSENCE

Throughout this book, I have authentically shared my life story to demonstrate that self-development and knowledge of one's own emotional conflicts are the keys to acquiring the authority to be seen, noticed, and fulfilled.

It is in BEING that I recognize myself as a person and realize that I can DO anything. From this, I recognize my merits in HAVING prosperity and developing my projects with the confidence to achieve desired results and personal fulfillment.

Have you heard of the pyramid of the individual?

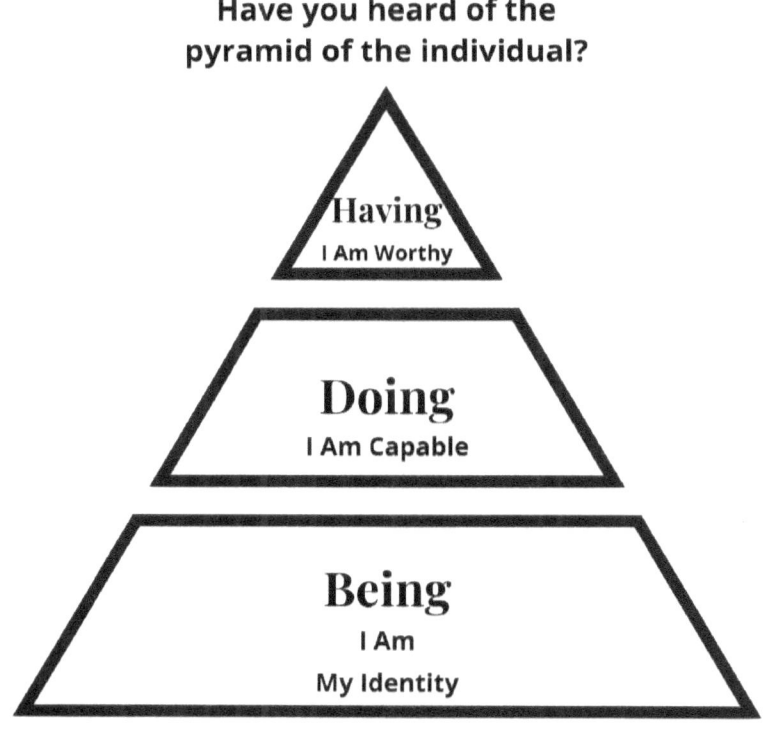

Having
I Am Worthy

Doing
I Am Capable

Being
I Am
My Identity

*Developed by Coach Paulo Vieira.

By truly understanding the concept of resilience, I can choose the paths I want to travel with assertive choices, away from anything that harms me in any way, and make decisions that are more aligned with my journey. However, the most important thing was to become aware that everything I experienced was necessary for me to understand the usefulness of each of these events, taking the opportunity to propel my life to even greater heights.

In bringing the "Salto Alto Connection" Project to life, I developed a method to help people connect more deeply with themselves, leverage effective life strategies, and ultimately achieve financial prosperity.

The project was based on the triad of the following powers: **authenticity, self-development**, and **authority** to offer a structured approach and stimulate the growth of each participant, mainly because of the profound impact on personal advancement.

However, the Salto Alto method is not just a model for individual transformation but a catalyst for social change. You don't evolve in isolation when you embark on this journey full of embracing, mutual help, and personal transformation. Each person's growth has a cascading effect, influencing the relationships you participate in more broadly.

Promoting this development enables people to become more active in society, experience authentic journeys, and live a life full of enthusiasm and success. It instigates positive change and inspires others to follow their own paths of development.

By cultivating a powerful and valuable mindset, the "Salto Alto Connection" method embraces principles such as discipline and action to see life's challenges as learning opportunities rather than impossible obstacles.

This change in perspective is crucial for personal and professional development. It generates a commitment to learning and self-improvement, which can lead to innovation and creativity in various fields.

With this, the method is more than a set of principles, powers, and actions. It is a movement towards a more conscious and connected world. An invitation to embark on a journey of self-discovery, creating a more authentic identity in the development of the individual journey. Each leap gains greater momentum towards a bright and inclusive future.

The First Power: Authenticity

Just as in my personal story, it was only after I accepted my emotions that I made valuable connections that added to my transformation. I saw others without judgment, which strengthened my confidence and opened up space for new learning.

The act of embracing is extremely transformative, as it instigates the feeling of being part of something, while receiving others for who they are, seeing the value of their unique journey, full of choices, ideas, desires, and valid individual preferences. Authenticity is nothing more than being crystal clear with your real image, choices, behaviors, emotions, and journey.

As a power within the method, authenticity has the role of understanding the initial complaint of each participant and understanding which directions would be most aligned with their maximum potential. It is a powerful instrument for access and fair exchange because the basis of personal growth and the journey of self-improvement begins with honesty and the understanding of one's most authentic preferences.

Because it is a power that emphasizes the importance of creating a supportive and accepting understanding of what is natural to you, one can cultivate faith in their potential and the courage to face fears. Acceptance of one's current state, healthy self-esteem, and respect for one's personal preferences lay the foundations for authentic self-formation.

As authenticity is part of my journey, I established something that I instinctively noticed from the start of creating the method, and as I delved deeper into it. I then developed the following branches:

a) Faith

This topic focuses on belief in the process and its positive results. It's about fostering confidence in the method and the ability to bring about change. It's not about religion, but rather the powerful force that faith generates in developing one's abilities and expressing authentic preferences.

b) Courage

Courage involves facing challenges and leaving the comfort zone, the first leap towards real personal transformation. With courage, we have the strength to face fears and personal obstacles. With help, this strength sets us in motion, and we direct this movement towards a path that is more aligned with ourselves.

c) Trust

Trust is a crucial component of any welcoming environment, as it generates deeper and fairer connections, which build a foundation of trust and integrity, ensuring that the person feels safe. We are in this life to hold hands, not go alone. The only way to go through it together is to trust oneself, the journey, and those who hold our hands.

d) Acceptance

Acceptance means recognizing and embracing the current

state of things or personal circumstances. It is an attitude of non-resistance and openness to new experiences.

e) Self-esteem

Self-esteem is related to one's perception of self-value, making one more confident to make great leaps in transformation and self-validation of choices, preferences, and desires. This acceptance stimulates a higher self-esteem, not in the sense of vanity but self-respect.

f) Preferences

This branch is extremely important because recognizing the individuality of choices and tastes allows us to align our journey with our most authentic purpose. Everyone has an evolutionary process, and we need to respect personal preferences. Clarity about personal preferences stimulates progression with more enthusiasm and takes increasingly high and effective leaps.

The Second Power: Self-Development

By understanding that we have value, we transform the energy that would otherwise be used to judge and compete into unity and help. Thus, self-development is structured within a knowledge acquisition framework that goes from the inside out. It starts with self-knowledge and expands to skills, focus, preferences, and goals. By lucidly aligning these stages, we can act more effectively and take higher leaps in life.

As one prepares to embark on a growth journey, self-development provides the necessary tools and guidance through knowledge, resulting in enabling informed decisions. At the same time, effective communication ensures that needs are understood and met.

Building connections with other people creates a support network, which is essential for facing life's challenges, especially by recognizing the power of choices and the ability to overcome adversity as fundamental in this phase of change. Additionally, drawing on different forms of intelligence enables a more adaptable approach to problem-solving.

Here, the focus is on providing practical support and multidisciplinary resources that enable the person to solve problems. To this end, based on knowledge and experience, this power provides resources such as emotional tools, connections, and discussions that favor the resolution of the demand. This structured support intervention fosters personal transformation and authority development.

In this power, the following strategic branches of action have been developed:

a) Knowledge

It emphasizes the importance of information and the complete understanding of the parts involved in a development process, all in a structured way so that there is an educational process from the inside out (the basis of self-empowerment). No fear can resist knowledge, just as there is no evolution without experience. Experience is nothing more than applied knowledge. In this power, we encourage focused acquisition and effective application so that each person's path yields useful results.

b) Communication

Effective communication is fundamental to providing help,

understanding preferences, and mapping out action strategies that generate more appropriate results in the individual or collective search for self-development. This starts with a clear, open dialogue about understanding needs and offering a more effective language structure. Communication happens in different ways, and we need to know the importance of verbal and non-verbal in building strong connections.

c) Connection

Connections are necessary for self-development and personal transformation through authenticity. Building strong relationships is essential for effective self-development, not just stronger, trustworthy relationships, but also fair exchanges and strategies. By developing valuable connections, we expand our network and create a system of mutual support and assistance.

d) Choices

We have the power to change the course of our journey at any time. To do so, we must recognize and respect individual choices that are aligned with authentic preferences and purposes. In the power of choice, we give tone to our experiences and create outcomes that align us on a more just and satisfying path, while also empowering us to positively impact our surroundings.

e) Overcoming

Overcoming means overcoming obstacles, getting back on your feet after falls, forgiving what has happened, and moving on stronger and wiser. This perseverance with the process allows for greater flexibility and resilience. It involves overcoming difficulties and transforming them into opportunities for growth and self-development, since it involves the shadows and beliefs that can get in the way of a fairer path.

f) Intelligence/Strategy

Intelligence is not just about the cognitive ability to learn but also the ramifications of emotional, social, and strategic intelligence. By understanding these differences, we can find more effective strategies for helping ourselves, deepening our understanding of ourselves, and transforming ourselves through self-development.

Intelligence is a learning capacity connected to strategy, knowledge application, and understanding experiences. When in harmony with fluid emotional intelligence, this logical-strategic ability allows for high resilience and the potential to develop strength through wisdom.

The Third Power: Authority

When we understand who we are and what direction we want to take in our journey, we take actions, behaviors, and mental and emotional processes that manifest our more authentic and abundant version of life.

The final power of the "Salto Alto Connection" method deals with the change and growth that occur when one evolves through the previous powers, mainly because the goal shows progression.

Authority is the true metamorphosis that takes place through discipline, deliberate and strategic actions to begin to achieve our goals.

Authenticity throughout the process ensures that changes are genuine and align with one's values and preferences. At the same time, empowerment provides the confidence to take control of one's destiny. Trust and faith provide the strength to wisely overcome setbacks in decision-making, ensuring that each leap is taken more effectively.

This power aims to facilitate significant changes in our lives, as it focuses on transforming the journey from a current state of lack of enthusiasm and alignment to a future of success and abundance in various layers of life.

It's natural to amplify the positive impact generated because it comes with results, language, help, and security. All this power generates authority over oneself and one's own path.

Personal growth occurs through the development of skills, the application of acquired knowledge, the creation of focus strategies, and the expansion of one's notion of oneself.

"Salto Alto Connection" seeks to incentivize, guide, instrumentalize, and support possible and fair improvements. Therefore, this power branches out into the following points:

a) Discipline

It is the practice of training oneself to follow a behavior or choice that is more aligned with one's own journey. This is possible by applying routine actions and strategies to achieve consistent transformations in results, well-being, health, professional success, relationships, and other areas of life.

b) Action

It's the process of doing something to achieve an objective. We know transformation only happens when actions are rethought, adapted, and effective. This movement needs direction since we can only align actions that generate more satisfactory results.

c) Honesty

This branch is one of the most important in the process of personal transformation because only by being clear about our choices can we achieve great leaps in life. Self-acceptance provides the opportunity for a fuller and more enthusiastic life. With honesty, we can reduce judgments, see our abilities and preferences, and eliminate limiting beliefs and emotional processes of denial.

d) Empowerment

Empowerment is nothing more than gaining the strength and confidence to take control of your own life. With all the previous branches, authenticity, and self-development, we can make great leaps of transformation through personal empowerment. This empowerment does not instigate the illusion of pride, but rather, clear and effective authority over one's abilities and path.

e) Resilience/Coping

It's the ability to recover from difficulties and overcome obstacles without getting lost. Resilience provides a breath of consistency and strategic coherence in maintaining our choices and transforming ourselves into a more authentic, aligned, and authoritative version.

f) Wisdom

Acquiring knowledge broadens our skills and aligns our actions for better results. The consistency of the process makes us wiser because there is no real wisdom without results. While it's common for many people to seek knowledge, this doesn't bring results unless it is applied, triangulated, and experienced.

Each power connects to the previous one, creating a more comprehensive approach. It can be applied to various contexts, such as personal development, organizational change, or community impact work. It is therefore a method not only of personal development but also of social entrepreneurship.

Salto Alto Connection proves the power of structured help

and the intentional action of embracing. Even with the complexity of individual growth in its emotional, cognitive, and practical aspects, the method promotes a culture of self-development that values personal empowerment and each person's impact on the environment. As I've mentioned, Salto Alto is not about shoes but our lives and the potential to help each other evolve as a society.

It's worth noting that the *Salto Alto Connection* training method recognizes the potential of each participant, as it's grounded in the values of honor, respect, responsibility, help, support, honesty, and unity. We know that we can achieve much more when we join hands and help each other.

Conclusion

This book represents the blueprint for a long process of self-development and emotional maturity that I have followed in my life journey, and you have read on every page.

There have been many adversities, difficulties, and moments when I completely disbelieved in my ability to transform. Today, I can say that every day, I learn a little more and prepare myself for higher leaps with the authority of someone who is and does what she says, who knows how to join hands and grow with those who, by fate, join hands with me, too.

In every talk I give, I demonstrate how faith and overcoming are powerful tools within each of us. Thanks to my faith, I haven't let myself get lost on unvirtuous paths or in myself. Today, I acknowledge my strength and authority, and appreciate the connections in my personal and professional circles.

My main goal with "Salto Alto Connection" is to positively

impact people's results and lives. I welcome their needs and provide knowledge so that they can deal with emotional issues in a harmonious, authentic, and effective way.

As I work with the training groups and my own experience, the project expands further, creating new connections while maintaining its essence. The possibility of developing the work online has further expanded the range of people involved, including both participants and professionals.

The last edition brought together women from Brazil, the United States, and other countries in a powerful connection of resilience. It still continues to grow with editions in Switzerland and other American states.

I am on the right track for all these reasons. Believing in my dreams and desire to build something significant for the world was worth it.

"Salto Alto Connection" will soon have its own book presenting the new, updated, and expanded structure. Humans constantly evolve and learn, and we cannot limit our potential.

"Salto Alto Connection" follows this same principle and will continue to evolve so we can help each other more. I believe that life is about growing and contributing.

So here's my invitation.
Are you ready for the biggest leap of your life?

· Testimonials

Mari Lopes
São Paulo

"When I met Cleo a few years ago, she became a key player in transforming my behavior. In addition to being generous and full of love, Cleo is a strong, caring, and extremely disciplined woman. She has the gift of changing our perspective on life by bringing insights that really make a difference. In this process, I lost 55 pounds, but what matters is the profound transmutation that took place in my mind, both physically and spiritually. Cleo was a real turning point in my journey, and I am eternally grateful for this incredible woman who transforms lives while keeping her essence pure and unique."

Sheyla Aguiar
São Paulo

"When God planned our meeting, he used his greatest gift: communication. I heard you for the first time through communication, and we found each other through it. Your wise advice helped me reconnect with myself and my essence while recovering my self-love, [and] personal, and professional development."

· Testimonials

Chloe Gomes
Long Island, New York

"Do you see this woman full of self-esteem and certainty that everything will work out? She didn't exist before several changes and opportunities, one of them being Cleo Pillon and "Salto Alto Connection". When you're in a group that supports you, believes in your dreams, understands your pain, and makes you believe you can achieve everything you set out to do, you become unstoppable! Grateful for everyone involved! Thank you, "Salto Alto Connection"! Thanks, Cleo!"

Debora Manfre
Long Island, New York

"Taking part in "Salto Alto" was a truly transformative experience. Cleo has a simple and straightforward way of teaching, which truly impacts our mentality. Her story of resilience is inspiring and shows us that we can build the life of our dreams. I'm immensely grateful, Cleo, for everything you deliver and for motivating us to believe in our potential."

Monica Grecco
New Jersey

"Cleo and I met through a mutual friend. Our first contact was by voice memo. Right from the start, I noticed something different in her voice. A tranquillity that I couldn't explain, mainly because I had never seen Cleo before. As the days passed, we exchanged more voice memos, and the peace she transmitted caught my attention the most. During one of these conversations, we talked about resilience. In the end, I mentioned how, after my mother's death, I was no longer able to pray and how much that bothered me. Cleo, with her welcoming manner, looked into my eyes and said: 'How about we pray? ' That prayer rekindled something in me. A flame that had been extinguished. And I noticed that what prevailed at that moment was her concern in reminding me how special I am and that I was only grieving. Cleo, with her wisdom and generosity, always shares something valuable. I am immensely grateful for our friendship and for having someone so special by my side."

· Testimonials

Priscila Carreon
New Jersey

"Connecting people is Cleo's natural and inherent talent. When necessary, she gets up on a stage and handles it. Those most intimate know how what she does behind the scenes has an immeasurable impact on the lives of those who have the privilege of crossing their path. The overflow for her is uncontrollable and makes everyone around her take great leaps. I doubt her story won't impact and motivate everyone who will have the privilege of accessing it."

Ana Paula P. Caldas
Connecticut, USA

"Cleo, a woman of unshakeable faith, can transform any environment by bringing joy and her welcome. Just as it says in Proverbs 31:10: A virtuous woman, who will find her? She is worth far more than rubies. Cleo is a treasure I have found, a friend who welcomes me with the warmth of a home, and inspires me to seek a deeper faith—a woman who, even amid diversity, manages to transmit peace. I admire her constant search to be closer to Christ and feel inspired. That's what I admire most about her."